DAY *HUSTLE*™

Receive the Benefits of a DAY Job
While You Grow Your Side *HUSTLE*

G. M. RAHMANI

Day Hustle™ Copyright 2022 G. M. Rahmani

For more information, e-mail mediarelations@dayhustlers.com.
ISBN Paperback: 979-8-9867733-0-8
ISBN Hardcover: 979-8-9867733-1-5
Library of Congress Control Number: 2022917036

DEDICATION

This book is dedicated to the people who can't make ends meet, who have to miss their son's first steps or their daughter's softball game for work, who loses their job to a robot, or who struggles to take care of the people who took care of them.

This book is for the people who work 12 hours a day, five days a week to make someone else rich, or who work 18 hours a day, seven days a week to make themselves rich.

This book is for the people itching to pursue their passion and follow their dreams, "one day."

This book is for the people who seek freedom, but who are too afraid to turn the key that they, themselves, hold.

TABLE OF CONTENTS

FOREWORD

I first met Gianna in what I thought was going to be a routine new client meeting in my Florida law office. The meeting turned out to be anything but routine. Gianna, supported by her husband, Farhad, wasted no time and jumped headlong into her story, ideas, and concepts with passion and excitement. After an hour and a half of intense discussions, I walked away highly impressed with Gianna's plan, her questions, level of preparation, and original thought. She is a one-of-a-kind business owner with an excellent idea, and a plan to make it happen. I should know. I have worked with hundreds of them.

As a business attorney, I have formed more startup companies than I can number, and I have worked with every type of entrepreneur. I know firsthand how difficult starting your own business can be. I have seen startups succeed, startups fail, and I have seen many many startups never even start. There are many reasons for this, but usually the entrepreneur could not find a way to separate themselves from their day job, or juggle both a full-time job and their side hustle. I cannot number the amount of clients I have helped through the years who shelved their newly formed company within the first year because they could not dive in or balance the extra workload that starting a new business brings.

The concept behind Day Hustle™ is as original as it is powerful because it solves the basic problem that almost every startup faces – how can you devote full-time attention to the startup when the new business does not have enough revenue to cover your living expenses?

I have worked alongside Gianna over the weeks and months since our first meeting, drafting the necessary contracts, developing ideas, and making Day Hustle™ a reality. I can honestly say that Gianna's concept has the capacity to change lives for millions of people struggling to find their best life and financial freedom.

Before walking into the large conference room where I met Gianna and Farhad for the first time, my paralegal told me with a knowing smile, *"You are going to like this one."* She was right! For all entrepreneurs looking for a way to make their dreams reality, I enthusiastically recommend this book, Gianna's leadership, and the concept of Day Hustle™.

Jared A. Mangum, Esquire

PREFACE

If you were living the life of your dreams, how would you describe it? Do you see yourself sunbathing poolside, perhaps reading a book while drinking your favorite cocktail, or on a fishing boat waiting for your next bite with a beer in your hand? Ever imagine yourself as CEO of a global company jet setting around the world or getting that Honma Golf Beres driver out at tee time? (Although I occasionally hit the greens, I have no idea what a *Honma Golf Beres* driver is. I Googled "most expensive golf driver!")

Do you visualize yourself on a mission trip abroad or within the country you live? Do you see yourself owning real estate, sports cars, and yachts, or do you envision yourself in an RV, on a motorcycle, or on a cruise ship? Do you foresee the freedom to work for *yourself* when and wherever you want so you can do whatever makes *you* happy and spend time with the people you love?

The person I love the most is my husband, and if I'm going to go by G, let's call him F – after all *F Words are My Favorite* (check out my blog at fwordsaremyfavorite.com). My mission is to deliver a message of love through every word I speak (or write) and action I take, reflective of my favorite F words – Family, Fun, Faith, Fitness, Food, Finances, Freedom, and Fulfillment. What is your personal mission statement? I encourage you to write out a formal one if you haven't already.

While I may have written this book, note that the stories and statements are from both my husband's and my collective perspective as one unit, so "I" and "we" are used interchangeably. And if you sneak a peek at my vision board (I encourage you to make one of these, too, if you haven't already) you'll see pictures of F's and my honeymoon. Okay, Farhad. His name is Farhad – F just isn't one of the letters that sounds right as a nickname!

Farhad and I drove to two different places on our honeymoon – Angels Camp and Lake Tahoe. To be honest, these weren't what I had pictured as honeymoon destinations – no plane ride to a white sandy beach in the Bahamas or gondola ride in Venice – but I'll write about that another day.

Angels Camp is a small town in the Goldrush country of central California. As we drove into the town, the speed limit dropped drastically, and we were pulled over. Unfortunately, just getting married did not have a warming effect on the policeman who gave us a ticket, but we didn't let that damper our mood.

Fishing is nothing special to me, but my husband loves it and we always enjoyed going fishing together before, so we went fishing at Angels Camp, too. We picnicked on the banks of the lake. I hooked my own creepy crawlers and napped under the sun. We rented a boat there and my favorite picture from our honeymoon was of Farhad driving it with the wind blowing through his hair.

After a few days at Angels Camp, we got into our rented Dodge Intrepid and headed towards Tahoe. Unbeknownst to us, a huge blizzard had already covered the mountain in a foot of snow, and it was still coming down by the time we were on it. Without even having chains on our tires, Farhad will never forget the long and slow trek up the mountain, as he passed by a few *four-wheel drives* being towed back up off the edges! I, not surprisingly, was napping for most of it.

Eventually, we made it to the Heavenly Ski Resort. Farhad had only snowboarded before, and I had only skied in the past. Thinking how much cooler (and hotter *winky face*) Farhad was snowboarding, I decided to give it a shot. After several hours of trying to make it to the bottom, I fell for what seemed like the hundredth time and got the wind knocked out of me so badly that I had to have the "ride" of shame down the rest of the mountain on a snowmobile.

Let's call it "F&G's Wild and Crazy Adventure," also known as our honeymoon and it was ah-mazing! You may think we're crazy (and maybe we are), but that's what living the life is for us and we're definitely not going to judge you for what you envision for your dream life.

But it's just a phase, right? The honeymoon phase? While honeymoons vary in length, there are no rules, and we don't think it should be limited to a weekend, a week, or at all for that matter. If we want to live the life of our dreams, then we would let the honeymoon phase continue on and live *The Honeymoon Life* 'til death do us part.

I'm not talking about doing the same things or being at the same places as we did on our honeymoon. I'm talking about the *characteristics* that make a honeymoon so important in the first place, and you can even be *single* to appreciate most of them.

First, we traveled. We were on vacation having the time of our lives, and we weren't thinking about work or bills we had to pay. We were relaxed having no set schedule. While it was scary at times, it was fun and exhilarating. We were adventurous. This included trying new things and going places we've never gone before. We were wearing new outfits (at least I was), eating good food, and drinking. We were having lots of fun and had the freedom to do what we wanted.

As a couple, it's important to note that a honeymoon is a time that you purposely *want* and *plan* to be with each other. Newly married, we were "heart eyes" for each other, and head-over-heels in love. We were focused on each other and on making each other happy. We were patient with each other and quicker to forgive, we were doing things to impress each other, and while we were living in the moment, we were excited for the future. On our honeymoon, my husband and I were high on life and high on each other. It was date night every night, and we didn't want it to end.

The relationship stuff is always a work in progress and *The Honeymoon Life*, or whatever life you envision for yourself, will also take some creativity and hard work, especially if you want to create a life you don't need a vacation from. While I had made a lucrative career working for a few incredible companies and certainly enjoyed my paid vacations, they always had to end. They were always at the cost of returning to an inbox full of e-mails (those that didn't get answered while *on* vacation anyway) and a pile of work that would require another vacation to re-energize from. It was a never-ending cycle that I decided I wanted to break.

After reading several books and articles, watching several videos, listening to podcasts, studying various people, businesses, and websites, and countless hours of brainstorming and planning with my husband, I discovered job security was holding us back. I wished someone would pay me my salary so I could do my own thing. I've read and heard countless times that if I want something, then I have to give it away first. I never fully grasped this concept, but I do now, and that's what Day Hustle™ is all about.

THANK YOU for picking up this book. We don't know you personally, but this could be the start of a mutually beneficial relationship and we look forward to helping you live the life you envision while you, honestly, do the same for Farhad and me and allow us to live *The Honeymoon Life*!

Don't forget to recognize and deliver love today,

G

INTRODUCTION

This book is about day jobs and side hustles, but more importantly, it's about receiving the benefits of a day job while you grow *your* side hustle. Day Hustle™, LLC is a company willing and able to match the right candidate's salary from their current day job, offer health insurance and access to other group coverage, as well as a 401k retirement plan – all this for the sole purpose of growing your own business.

In other words, it's about job security without the job – it's *life* security, as we discuss later. Day Hustle™ does not sell any goods or services for which it requires research, product, or business development nor does it have any customers to represent or service; thus, it is not looking for employees to support *itself,* but rather for employees to find support for *themselves.* Day Hustle™ is an equal opportunity employer, and everyone is encouraged to apply.

Day Hustle™ is the *original* angel employer™. Angel employment™ is being introduced by Honeymoon Media to the world through the launch of this book. As such, the reading and understanding of this book is required of every candidate. This book is filled with questions for you to think about, as it is important to answer them for yourself. If, after reading this book and answering the questions posed inside, you feel like you deserve to be a day hustler™, then you will be ready to complete a majority of the application.

If you are not looking for employment, but rather interested in this new form of private equity/business investing, then do continue reading. Angel employment™ is in its infancy. Reading this book will help you fully grasp the concept and understand the key side of the deal – our day hustlers™.

There's a section in *Make Your Own Luck*, a book by Bob Miglani and Rehan Yar Khan, that is summarized as follows: *"It's about them, not about you. If you want to speed up the level of success in your life, find out what people want and find a way to give it to them. Give with the intention to help."* This said, I do address you and your role as an investor in the bonus chapter – *Angel Employment*™ *Explained*. We have an opportunity to help millions of people grow successful businesses and live fulfilling lives, and I can show you how!

CHAPTER ONE

THE BASICS OF DAY JOBS AND SIDE HUSTLES

"Do not let making a living prevent you from making a life." John Wooden

---

T he reason I'm starting this book with the basics is that I realize everyone is not only at different points in his or her life, but we all have different understandings of certain subject matters. Take "surviving" and "living" as examples. Both of these will be addressed in upcoming chapters. Each of us also defines success, the perfect job, the dream life, and freedom differently. Retirement is another great example of a subject that some folks have different understandings of. I'm not going into all the possible definitions because there are too many. I've read lists with the 14 "best" definitions and some with as high as 36. I've read lists of all the "legal" definitions. And I've read articles that describe three "types" of retirement, while another article argues there are five. Personally, my favorite is punkybruster17's definition found in the *Urban Dictionary*, *"When your tired one day and your tired again the next. This is called being retired."* I love a good dad joke!

In this book, I refer to at least two perspectives on retirement – the first is when someone becomes eligible for retirement benefits from a retirement plan, such as a 401k, or from the government in the form of Social Security (the various lists of *examples* of retirement benefits completely blow the lists of definitions out of the water).

The second is when someone chooses to leave the "workforce" behind "permanently." Now, we've all seen famous athletes that have come out of retirement, and we've all heard the expressions about doing things you love and never working a day in your life. To me, workforce refers to employees – the people that work for someone else to earn a wage or salary – to "make a living."

What if I were to ask what you do for a living? I know that there are countless jobs and professions out there. According to *Indeed,* the most common jobs in America in 2021 ranged from working as a cashier, administrative assistant, bookkeeper, mechanic, registered nurse, marketing specialist, operations manager, lawyer, and software developer. This article not only lists 25 jobs and describes the worker's primary duties, it also notes the national average salary for each position. By reading the article, it appears that the jobs are listed in order of salary, as opposed to the number of jobs in America, so that's important to note. The salaries ranged from $10.84 per hour to $93,303 per year. What do you make for a living?

Day Jobs

When someone asks you what you do for a living, you typically talk about your day job, the regular work you do to earn your primary source of income. A day job was often referred to as a "nine-to-five," a colloquial expression that came from the time Henry Ford, founder of the Ford Motor Company, introduced the concept of the eight-hour day, 40-hour workweek to prevent his assembly line workers from burning out. He was a hero to the many Americans working 10-to-12-hour shifts performing tedious manual labor for 60+ hours a week. Typical business operating hours are from nine o'clock in the morning to five o'clock in the evening. What are your work hours?

While times have changed, a person's day job can extend into the evening, be spread throughout the day and night (especially for remote work environments), or even be overnight. The expression still refers to the work you do to earn your ordinary income. At the minimum, these wages hopefully cover your basic necessities such as housing, food, transportation, healthcare, and taxes. Does your day job cover your essentials?

Side Hustles

A day job is the work someone does to "make a living." Unfortunately, *living* is on the other side of the day job. And that's where the *side* hustle comes in. A side hustle is a job that people have, a project that people pursue, and/or a business that people run in addition to, or *aside* from, their primary responsibilities, whether they are attending school, raising children, or working a day job.

In the first example, you may think of Elon Musk, notorious for running a nightclub out of his college house at the University of Pennsylvania to pay for his rent, or Mark Zuckerberg who worked on developing social platforms while attending Harvard, including the platform that later would be known as Facebook. Under Armour also started while Kevin Plank was playing football for the University of Maryland.

Unless you turn it into a daycare facility, raising your own children typically doesn't generate any income, so moms, dads, and/or guardians may turn to a side hustle to help cover expenses. And while the day job often provides the household's primary source of income, many people turn to a side hustle to supplement their salary.

A side hustle could be a money-making hobby like retail arbitrage, publishing books, and selling arts and crafts or baked goods. A side hustle could also be gig jobs, which are temporary or freelance work. Examples of gig work are driving for Uber or delivering for DoorDash, babysitting, and designing book covers through Fiverr, Upwork, or Reedsy. You could do a combination of both a hobby and a gig like personal training for those that enjoy exercise and nutrition, or photography businesses. The side hustle could be musical or acting gigs where the goal is to become professional performers – in these cases, the day job is meant to be the supplemental income that supports that objective. Other side hustlers often start businesses related to their profession like bookkeeping by accountants and tutoring by teachers. Others may sell for network marketing companies like Amway, Mary Kay, Beach Body, LuLaRoe, and Pampered Chef. Side hustlers are also often investors who trade stocks, flip real estate, or rent out space on AirBnB.

Entrepreneurs who take a creative idea for a product or service and take the risk of starting their own business may begin as side hustlers. It takes time to get their invention or solution to profit, so entrepreneurs often work long hours, waking up early, doing their day job, only to work on their side hustle once they clock out, all before going to bed late. However, these business founders could turn their startup into a company that eventually goes public. The possibilities are endless with entrepreneurs, but they have to start from somewhere.

In terms of social media, we already talked about Facebook, borne out of a college dorm room. Instagram also started as a side hustle for Kevin Systrom and Twitter was a side project by Jack Dorsey.

Side hustles can be in any field or industry like technology, fashion, and education. Steve Jobs and Steve Wozniak created the first Apple computer in a garage. Sara Blakely was a salesperson by day and worked on her patent for Spanx at night. Sal Khan's day job was at a hedge fund, while Khan Academy started as a side hustle for tutoring his family members part-time.

More and more people are turning to side hustles for more and more reasons that we'll cover later in this book (understandably, people have different personal reasons, but there are major global/systemic reasons why everyone *should* go into business themselves). According to the Smarts Company's *2021 Side Hustle Statistics: Trends and Data*, *"Two-thirds (67%) of Americans who have a side hustle started it in the last three years, and nearly one-third (31%) started in 2020. As the data shows, one-third of Americans (34%) currently have a side hustle. In 2021, 61.1 million Americans (24%) intend to start a side hustle."* Do you have a side hustle? If not, do you have an idea for one?

As entrepreneurs grow their side hustles or as artists catch their big breaks, they eventually leave their day jobs. For those that see their side hustle simply as a hobby or as a source of supplemental income, however, they don't necessarily have the intention of working for themselves full-time. Once we discuss the main reasons why *everyone* should think about working for themselves, they should all start with a side hustle until they make it profitable enough to cover what they make from their day jobs. If you were Jeff Bezos, you'd quit your job and start Amazon. But you're not Jeff Bezos. Most people are afraid to quit their job, and this book is for those people.

Chapter Two

Reasons Why You Should Turn to Side Hustles

"Only a life lived for others
is a life worthwhile." Albert Einstein

Cost of Living

Whether your day job covers your personal basic necessities or not, you may have others to take care of as well – your kids, aging parents, and/or disabled family members. Who are your dependents? If you are not making enough from your day job, then you are not alone. Making ends meet is one of the biggest reasons that Americans have side hustles. This was before inflation reached 9.1% in June of 2022, the highest since the 80s. Prices are skyrocketing at the gas pump and at the grocery store. Housing costs are through the roof in many areas, no pun intended. Premiums on health, car, and property insurance are increasing exponentially. While premiums are increasing, are employers meeting the "standard of living" salary increases? Maybe. But what does that mean? They'll have to raise the cost of their goods and/or services to afford their employees (if they don't turn to shrinkflation, that is). Unfortunately, employees are also consumers having to spend more and more on less and less.

Fortunately, many side hustles can start by working from home, allowing you to save on gas and providing opportunities for appropriate business tax deductions advised by your tax preparer. According to Side Hustle Nation's *2022 Side Hustle Statistics and Survey Results*, the most popular and highest paying side hustles include online businesses and investing, which can often be started at home. The $10k+ per month side hustle earners are investing in real estate, cryptocurrency, stocks, and businesses.

Debt

Are you trying to pay off debt? While there are good kinds of debt that make you money, bad debt sucks money out of your pocket, and you can find yourself in a deep hole. It's important to get out of debt as soon as possible and stay out. What kind of debt do you have and how much do you owe? What steps are you taking to pay off your debt and when do you expect to have it paid off completely? Managing and maximizing the money you do make is crucial, especially when you are working both a day job and a side hustle to make it. These include using systems such as paying off your credit cards every month (and using those that earn you cash back like the CitiDouble Cash Card), credit monitoring, using an app to stay on budget, such as the Goodbudget app, or apps to get discounts and earn cash back like GetUpside, and using software like Quickbooks for bookkeeping. What systems, apps, and software do you use to manage your money?

Monetized Hobbies

Is your side hustle one that made sense to monetize? Life is about doing what makes you happy. Obviously, your hobby is something you enjoy doing enough to do it regularly. It makes sense (more than *cents*) to make money out of it. Earlier, I used the examples of retail arbitrage for people that love to shop, personal training for people that love to work out, and publishing books. I, for one, love writing. I also love helping people, and here we are. Just make sure to stay within the Internal Revenue Service's hobby loss rules and criteria.

Wants vs. Needs

Do you have a side hustle for the extra income to be able to watch a professional baseball game with your kids, to buy yourself a sports car, or to take your spouse to Hawaii? The specifics are different for everyone, but typically it's to afford to do something, buy something, or go somewhere. Most people see these as their wants, not their needs. In simple terms, there's a big difference between needing something and wanting something. Your basic expenses are what you need to survive. Anything else would be nice to have, and multiple streams of income helps us attain them. What are your wants? Other than your day job and your side hustle(s), what are your other sources of income?

Yes, your "cost of living" may be what you need to survive, but are you truly *living* if all you are doing is surviving? Let's call them surviving expenses from here on out. You can't take a shower, leave home, gas up, drive to work, work all day, pay taxes on the money you earned from working all day, pay the water bill for that shower you took, pay for your car and gas to get to that job, and pay your rent or mortgage and/or property taxes, just to do it all over again the next day. That is not *living*, in my opinion. Living is experiencing what this world has to offer while you're vibrant enough to enjoy it. You *need* to live as much as you need to survive. Your wants are just as important as your needs.

In other words, it would be nice to have what you want, but you wouldn't be truly living if you didn't have it. What would make you feel *alive*? If you have a strong enough reason – your "why" they call it – you'll find that *needing* to reach your goals, whatever they may be, is the motivation you need to keep hustling. What is your "why?"

Retirement Planning

Are you investing your side hustle income to supplement your 401k? If you didn't start retirement planning early enough, you may not have enough money to live once you retire. Social Security is depleting rapidly with baby boomers retiring. Since many people are turning to working for themselves, there aren't enough new employees paying into the system. Some economists are expecting Social Security funds to be exhausted by 2034. Imagine working all of your life, then when you are finally done with your day job, you don't have enough money to live. It's a sad but possible reality for many of us.

I know of some that have diligently worked a quarter of a century for a company known for its great benefits, including its retirement plan. However, as they approach retirement age, they are preparing to live under a fixed income less than what it would take to live comfortably, let alone thrive. With no other choice, they are forced to continue working the number of hours required to stay eligible for the health benefits the company provides. If they are fortunate enough, they may have children to take care of them, but if their children did not plan on investing in long-term senior care for the chance their mother and/or father would need it, there either won't be any professional care available when they do need it, or the level of the plan would depend on the children contributing "what they can afford." Their parents' future care should not be based on this after all of the love they have given to, and sacrifices they have made for, their children. Fortunately, it's not too late for you or your parents, if you hustle, that is.

Freedom

Are you side hustling for the purpose of working for yourself, to build wealth, and to be financially free? Being your own boss is attractive to many people – there's no one to tell you what to do, and you have the freedom to do things your way. According to Side Hustle Nation's survey, "*the PRIMARY motivation to start (or seek information about)*" a business or side hustle was personal freedom. This freedom leads to money that results in more freedom, like financial freedom.

Here is a quote from the book *The Psychology of Money* by Morgan Housel – "*The ability to do what you want when you want, with who you want, for as long as you want, is priceless. It is the highest dividend money pays.*" Working for yourself is the way to build wealth. If you haven't already, then you should definitely read Robert Kiyosaki's series of books, including *Rich Dad, Poor Dad*, *Cashflow Quadrant*, and *Rich Dad's Guide to Investing*. Reading all three of these books changed my husband's and my perspective and, in turn, changed our life forever. I'm on the fast track to financial freedom and my goal is to become financially free by the time I turn 40. There are many people that have become financially free much sooner, while several made it big after the age of 65, like Colonel Sanders, the founder of KFC. Your goal should be your own. I, personally, plan to do it sooner than later so that I can enjoy The Honeymoon Life now, while I'm young and, thankfully, healthy.

What are your reasons for your side hustle?

Chapter Three

Reasons Why You Should Quit Your Day Jobs

"Working hard for something we don't care about is called stress; working hard for something we love is called passion."

Simon Sinek

B y now, you're hopefully convinced that a side hustle is important to pursue, but maybe not to the point of working for yourself completely. Let's explore why a day job is something you should *work to break free and escape* from.

Your Dream Job vs. Your Dream Life

First, are you doing what you love? For example, I enjoyed my job in business development and operations, but I would rather get paid to write, and to write what I want to write about. You may enjoy what you do at your day job, but are you *genuinely* pursuing your passion, is it giving you a *true* sense of fulfillment, or is there anything else that you would *love* to do instead? Secondly, are you working with the people you love, or at least like, and surrounding yourself with positive influences? Who are your mentors and role models? I was most certainly fortunate in this department, but lots of people do not like their boss, co-workers, or their customers. Thirdly, are you working within your *ideal* conditions or are you having to deal with (and settle for) *less*-than-ideal conditions, such as an inflexible schedule, office politics, and low pay. Big or small – what are the things you would change?

Perhaps you do have your dream job, but because you are working for someone else, whether you like them or not, you are not reaping the benefits of having your own business. People start working at different ages, many while still kids, but let's say they start when they turn 18. Let's also say they retire at 67 when full Social Security benefits are payable (if they were born 1960 or later). This is equal to 49 years. With an average 260 workdays a year, you could be working 12,740 days doing something you'd rather not be doing or doing something you love while making someone else rich!

You may think that the answer to this is to reduce the number of days you work for someone else, and you would be on the right track. What you also have to think about is that this may be done for you without you being prepared, and it's a race you may be losing. First, jobs are never completely secure – companies merge, get acquired, lay off workers, and fire unsuspecting employees all the time. Everyone was certainly surprised when Steve Jobs was kicked out of Apple.

My point is anything can happen. On top of this, we are currently in a world of entrepreneurialism, and various successful entrepreneurs are countering the need for services like formal education, given all the resources you need to learn may be available online. Who are teachers going to teach if no students show up? Teaching jobs are volatile and looking for alternative ways of teaching should have become a priority years ago. This is one example. As I reported earlier, more people are turning to side hustles and entrepreneurship. Don't be left out.

We are also in the world of advanced technology – namely, artificial intelligence (AI). While our world is going through a phenomenon called the "Great Resignation" with employees voluntarily resigning from their day jobs, they are also being laid off at alarming rates only to be replaced by AI and automation. Jobs in the following areas are projected to be made redundant: customer service, bookkeeping and data entry, food and retail, and courier and taxi services. These include many of the jobs listed in Chapter One and on *Indeed*'s list, so if those were the most common jobs, a lot of people are in trouble! According to *Saviom*, doctors, pharmacists, scientists, and soldiers are also at risk. And, while *Maverick* certainly couldn't be replaced, even the 2022 box office hit alluded to this impending inevitability.

Well, perhaps, being laid off is a blessing in disguise if it spurs you to start focusing on growing your own business.

Your day job is an *imaginary* safety net. The problem is, did you ever race or see someone race those obstacle courses where they climb a rope ladder or net? Your foot constantly gets stuck and it's a slow climb to the top. Job security is an illusion today, and we need to win this race now more than ever. We need *life* security. Better yet, we need our *dream* life security. The world soon may not need human employees, but it will always need the human spirit in the form of innovators, free thinkers, and entrepreneurs. Yes, there are lots of problems in today's world, but it has also generated millions of millionaires because problems need solutions.

I mentioned earlier that Social Security may be depleted by 2034. Before you receive your paycheck, 6.2% of your wages are taken out to fund a program that you may not see the benefit of. And Federal Insurance Contributions Act (FICA) taxes fund Medicare, which some have reported will run out even earlier than Social Security – many reports say 2026, but some say it could be as soon as this year (2022)! The current Medicare tax rate is 1.45% for the employee, so your total payroll tax is 7.65% of your paycheck. Now, you may be thinking that self-employment tax is twice that – very astute – but we'll address (and solve) that later in this book. Perhaps the government will intervene to acquire the necessary funding for these programs, but this could only mean more national debt, inflation, and/or higher tax rates. Before you receive your paycheck, federal, state, and/or local income taxes are also deducted, leaving very little for your surviving expenses (if even enough), let alone your *living* expenses.

My Dream Job

Thankfully, my day job was more than enough for both my surviving and living expenses. I may even say that my day job was like a golden goose. When I moved from Maryland, where I attended high school, to California to attend the University of California – Berkeley (UC Berkeley/Cal), I took a temporary job at a real estate and rental property management firm. It was only to stay busy and to make some money while waiting for my semester to start, but what I didn't realize then at 18 was that I would forever be in this industry (although in various capacities, even to this day). At that time, I worked as an administrative assistant and escrow coordinator – jobs that I enjoyed and excelled at. I also have to mention that I met my husband, Farhad, there, who was a rental property manager and real estate salesperson at the time. I worked alongside him and decided to get my real estate license to be able to work with him.

After withdrawing from UC Berkeley, getting married, earning a couple of associate degrees from a college no longer in existence, and having our first son, Nikolas, I moved back to Maryland with my new little family. I got back into real estate, working for $28k a year at a large firm as a branch administrator. And this was the start of my side hustling career – while many companies have employment policies to prevent conflicts of interest and the use of company computers for non-company-related use, "no moonlighting" policies mean you can't have a second job; however, because the pay was so low, our office manager/broker allowed me to offer marketing services to the agents who would individually and privately hire me to make flyers and brochures for them, and set up their websites. I worked there until I went on maternity leave for Farhad's and my second son, Dominik.

After a year and a half with the boys, I went back to work, this time in the community management sector of the real estate industry. I started as the assistant to three community managers, two of which were the company owners. As their assistant, I would go to sales presentations that they couldn't make until I took over the business development of the company. I was soon promoted to Director of Operations and Marketing, and again promoted to Vice President of the company. It wasn't necessarily side hustles here, but in the spirit of multiple income streams, I found ways to supplement my regular salary.

First, for the business development activities, I earned a commission for every new client I signed. Then, I helped them set up an affiliate maintenance company for which I earned a separate salary. Next, I helped them add a rental division from which I earned commissions for signing in new landlords until we eventually hired someone else to do the department's business development. Interestingly enough, it was my husband who they hired so it wasn't an actual loss of income for me. And because I spurred the new income stream for the company, I continued to earn commissions once units were leased. With the rental division up and running, Farhad and I assisted our employers in acquiring and merging with another rental company. This increased both our incomes. Then, our client landlords eventually wanted to use Farhad's services to sell their units, so this led to him obtaining his real estate broker's license to start a brokerage. You can bet your bottom dollar that we both took our cuts from those commissions as well.

I guess you would call me an *intrapreneur*, a term I recently learned from Patrick Bet-David of Valuetainment. As the years went by and as the company(ies) grew, my regular salary also increased, and on top of this, I earned residual income from the communities I signed for the company to manage. As I signed more and more, I received the initial sales commission, plus a percentage of the monthly management fees and, by the time I left 11 years into my tenure, I had been making money from communities every month since I signed them in. The funny story is, though it wasn't so funny at the time, I was careful in any documentation I had relating to my residual income.

It always said that I would continue to receive the income as long as the company managed the community, never stating that it would stop if I were to leave the company, and there's no law stating it had to be one way or another. Lo and behold, when I submitted my three months' notice (to relocate to Florida, another favorite F word of mine, by the way), I was informed that the payments would stop. I could have sought legal advice, but not only did I see them as family, I was also prepared to cut ties since the plan my husband and I had in place wasn't contingent on continuing to receive that income.

While I mentioned to them that that wasn't the deal, they confessed it was never the intention, which I both knew and understood – those payments were specifically set up to make it difficult for me to leave. I may have called it my golden goose but, luckily, the golden eggshells had cracks and I easily broke through.

While leaving such lucrative positions for both my husband and me seemed crazy for most, especially our employers, I didn't blame them for thinking that way and I was excited for the great things to come. At the time, I was uncomfortable to admit that I had already *secured* a replacement position with an even better pay package. After more than a decade working there, we grew close to a point that I expected probing questions about my new employer and new job that I wasn't ready to answer. This said, my husband and I have two boys to take care of. While we are bold in our decisions, nothing we do is done without serious thought and planning, and we had a great transition plan in motion. In Patrick Bet-David's keynote, *Think Like a Grandmaster Entrepreneur*, he recommends you always be prepared for your next *fifteen* moves.

Farhad and my plan *moved* us to Florida where we had decided we wanted to be seven years prior. Ironically, my husband and I flew to Florida as part of our job with our old employer in 2011. In reality, it was part of *my* job because we were going to a conference in the community association field, but it was my husband's first week with the company, so he got to tag along. We fell in love with Florida then, which we did not keep a secret, and the plan to relocate was set into motion. Rather than continuing to invest in property in Maryland, we put some of our money into a home in Florida and rented it out for the time being. When our tenants moved out, Nikolas was about to finish middle school, so it was the perfect time to move into our own rental – we'd figure out exactly where in Florida we want to be later, but this at least got us into the state.

As I mentioned, I already had my next day job lined up, but I asked them to wait for me to take the summer off. Our family took our time settling into our new home (we actually haven't completely settled in four years later because the house is only meant to be temporary while the boys finish high school). We went back to California for a couple of weeks and visited our old office where Farhad and I met, and this journey began. Knowing my new job was waiting for me, however, we flew back to Florida, got the boys going with their new schools, and I went to work.

This job was the best job I could ever ask for. I was based out of my home (way before COVID mind you) and worked on my own schedule. I was paid to have four-course meals, attend fancy parties, and tour resort-style communities. I got to travel all over Florida and explore our new home state with my husband and our two boys. Many people retire to Florida and that was the plan for Farhad. For us, retirement doesn't mean not doing anything. It means quitting our day jobs and working for ourselves, doing things we enjoy while building our wealth.

Since my day job covered more than our household surviving expenses, Farhad would take advantage of the time he had for himself to actively focus on adding to our assets (follow him on Instagram @activeretirement). The boys obviously had school and other activities, but on days off or over the 2020-2021 school year that they did fully virtually, you bet we were all together as I traveled to Jacksonville, Sarasota, Fort Lauderdale, Miami, and Cocoa Beach for work. I also even got to write for this job!

This job taught me so much in marketing, sales, systems, service, and leadership, and I learned from the best of the best. While I was certainly there for the income, the knowledge and experience I gained were priceless. I believe Robert Kiyosaki would be proud – *all* of the jobs I've had taught me a lot. But my last one did it differently. Before, they would rely on me to first figure things out, offer the ideas, and implement them, leading teams to carry forth our objectives. Here, it was backwards. I was placed on a team of highly intelligent, talented, motivated, and hardworking people led by incredibly smart, savvy, and caring executives. It was like graduating at the top of the class in middle school and transitioning as a freshman, but in a good way. This "school" taught me different ways of doing things as well as how to see and approach them.

Working with both peers and leaders at this level challenged me to grow to heights I wasn't able to before. This meant my commissions were on a whole new level. My first sale was double the size of my biggest at my prior job, and then the one following that was 8x this one. That's why I thought it would be fun to go by G. M. Rahmani – on top of some big-name authors like J. K. Rowling, C. S. Lewis, H. G. Wells, J. D. Salinger, and R. L. Stine, who I can only hope to be as influential as one day, I earned the nickname "G Money" from my team! Anyway, it was only after following their system that I was in a position to offer my own ideas, followed by a position where it was me they relied on to figure things out and help create systems for them. It was my last day job, and I had the great fortune that it was at such an incredible company. If you are looking to *learn* about marketing, sales, systems, service, and leadership, this is the company to work for!

Fool's Gold

Why would I leave my golden goose behind? In reality, day jobs are golden handcuffs, and I had to break free and escape. I never saw it this way before; never even heard the expression, to be honest, but as soon as I heard it, I knew that's exactly the situation I was in. Throughout my career, I've always had people approach me to convince me to leave whatever job I was at, at the time. I've never declined a conversation, always making it clear that I was under non-competes and confidentiality agreements, and strictly loyal to the company I was with.

This didn't deter them – they wanted me to hear what *they* had to say, and I would be a fool not to hear them out, if only to use what they said to increase my knowledge of the market and our competition. It was during one of these discussions where someone was offering me the opportunity to run my own operation – to finally be my own boss – that it started to click. I expressed to him how great I had it at my job and he called it my golden handcuffs. He was 100% right.

While my day job seemed perfect, it's just like every other day job out there, even yours. Even if you find a more efficient way of doing things and your systems are implemented, *at the end of the day*, you are always confined to how the company wants things done. You may be hired for a position that you enjoy in general, but *at the end of the day*, your company requires you to perform specific duties that you wouldn't necessarily choose to do. Your company may encourage fun and life balance – they may have parties and celebrations, and they don't "require" you to work on vacation. *At the end of the day*, you will be the one to deal with the ramifications of missing a call or letting your e-mails pile up until you return.

The good workers in every day job are always "rewarded" with more work since you are who they can rely on to get the job done and to do it right. This may lead to a promotion, but *at the end of the day*, your job responsibilities are further increased. Your salary may go up, but so do the taxes you pay. If a big percentage of your income is from commissions, the more you make means the even greater your employer makes. They may say that there is no ceiling for the income you earn, but *at the end of the day*, there is a limit, and the company will always find ways to impose these limitations. *At the end of the day,* you are enslaved to someone else's vision.

In my case, my compensation was undeniably increased when I did a good job. While the increases were rewards for a job well done, they are leverage to get even more out of me.

Even though I believed I deserved the increases for the work I did before the raise, I would always treat it as something I had to work even harder to earn after. The problem is, there are only 24 hours in a day for all of us. And as James Donnelly was quoted in the book, *The Formula for Luck* by Stuart Lacey, *"Every day is one less day, and my life is so incredible, I want to have one more day."*

If we don't put ourselves in a position where our money is working for us, even while we sleep, we'll never get the freedom to do what we want and when we want, and, most importantly, our days won't be as *incredible* as we want. We can only be as successful, rich, or free as we allow ourselves to be and no one else holds the key but ourselves, and it's at the end of the day *job*. Believing or accepting otherwise would be foolish.

Chapter Four

Reasons Why You Need to Move Quickly

"Your time is limited, so don't waste it living someone else's life. Don't be trapped by dogma – which is living with the results of other people's thinking." Steve Jobs

Fools Rush In

We're all fools to some extent. I've been a fool in love who rushed into marriage with someone two days short of eight months after meeting each other. Thankfully, what appeared to be a foolish teenager looks wiser and wiser every year. After 20 years of marriage, I can say with full confidence that marrying Farhad was the smartest decision I ever made. After 20 years of a "successful" career, however, I see the young, smart, energetic, and devoted employee that I have been only getting more foolish – if I didn't change anything that is.

Farhad has been listening to audiobooks for a long time. We'd often talk about the first one he listened to – *The 7 Habits of Highly Effective People* by Stephen R. Covey – ironically given to him by an old employer of his. I had always admired Farhad's discipline and how he seemed to multiply time. In the matter of hours it would take me to do one thing, he would accomplish a laundry list of tasks, a list that would still incorporate the seemingly unimportant tasks compared to his urgent and/or important objectives for that span of time.

He always makes the bed, for example, and checks off whatever else is on the "everyday" list, all while completing the project(s) he'd planned for that particular day, whether they are getting our dirt bikes ready for the track, creating a potato battery for Nikolas's science project, practicing ground balls with Dominik, doing a move-in inspection with a new tenant, dealing with the contractors at one of our flips, cooking a delicious Persian dinner, or all of the above!

Of the various work experiences Farhad has had, he also used to be a Mercedes-Benz Master Technician who would get paid on a flat rate. This meant that a specific job like changing brake pads would be paid based on a specific amount of time; let's say one hour. If he took longer than an hour, he wouldn't get paid any more than that. If he did eight brake jobs, but it took him 10 hours, he would only get paid for eight. True to his form, however, he would do 12 jobs in eight hours and get paid accordingly (the type of job and the number of them he did are examples). Anyway, my point in all of this is to say that Stephen Covey's book influenced Farhad and, after talking about the book several times and even listening to it once myself, it didn't click enough to make such an impact on me as it did him. While I get what needs to be done complete, I am nowhere near as disciplined as he is.

Over the years, Farhad continued to send me audiobooks and YouTube videos to listen to, and I did, at leisure, "watch" and "hear" them. I put these words in quotation marks because I wasn't "seeing" nor "listening" the way Farhad wanted me to. In 2018, he sent me Robert Kiyosaki's *Rich Dad, Poor Dad* audiobook. I heard it and noted some great points, but didn't do much with them.

First, it was interesting how Robert said he was a best "selling" author, not a best "writing" author. I actually started writing a book in 2016, but put it on hold for various reasons. The main reason was that I didn't know how to get the book into as many hands as possible. The book is about Farhad's and my secret to success (although I don't keep it a secret) as a couple, parents, best friends, and business partners. It is such an important message for me to share as I believe it will help people have happier and more fulfilling lives, and the point Robert made intrigued me. I thought that when I am "ready" to complete that book, when I don't have work in the way, I'll be sure to put a focus on the selling aspect as much as the writing.

Rich Dad, Poor Dad also made us look at spending and assets in a different way. Although we were doing quite well for ourselves, we could always do a lot better. We certainly found

Robert's key point of wisdom about our personal house *not* being an asset interesting and talked to the boys about it during one of our talks – we made it a point when they were both still in elementary and middle school to have "classes" and "meetings" with them about finances and investing and to keep them involved. After this book, I urged myself to listen to *Think and Grow Rich* by Napoleon Hill.

I've never been the type to fear bold moves and big changes, but that's only because I had good plans in place. What I got from this book, though, is that even if something doesn't work out later, I shouldn't be afraid of the possibility because if I keep pushing, eventually, I will find the real "gold." It was a great story and I heard these words, but clearly, I wasn't listening – nothing changed afterwards. During the 2020 quarantine, we got Robert Kiyosaki's *Cashflow 101* boardgame to teach the boys about money and how to get out of the "rat race," what he calls the proverbial hamster wheel keeping us from financial freedom. But, yet again, that's the extent to which we took it.

It wasn't until earlier this year that things changed for us. On January 30, 2022, Farhad texted me the YouTube link to *Rich Dad's Guide to Investing*, the third book in Robert Kiyosaki's series. On February 9th, I started to listen to it on my way to a work event. I recognized a lot of points that Robert was reinforcing from *Rich Dad, Poor Dad*, points I had only "heard" before. However, I had just turned 39 a week before, I was assigned another job responsibility the day before, and I was driving 234 miles for work that day. All the points I was "listening" to seemed to click.

Everything from this point until March 31st is a blur. (This will be fun – can you guess what happened on March 31, 2022?) I'll tell you why this date is a turning point later, but this 50-day period was a whirlwind of finishing the audiobook, conversations with Farhad and the boys about what do we do and where do we go from here, listening to several podcasts and YouTube videos, going back to listen to *Rich Dad, Poor Dad*, listening to the second book of the series, *Cashflow Quadrant,* and listening to the third book again! We wanted to listen to all three books together this time so that we could discuss exactly what points we related to, and had questions about. The sense of urgency was sparked (a flame that quickly burst into a wild blaze) and we were listening at every chance we got – over breakfast before work, in the car on the way to dinner, at baseball games (we'd share our earbuds in the stands), while working out, and on our trip to Arizona and the Grand Canyon. We actually stopped and took a selfie outside Rich

Dad's office in Phoenix because I knew one day, and one day soon the way things were going, we'd be telling our story about how his books changed our lives.

The Enlightened Hustle

Once I was "enlightened," I finally realized that the golden goose was a golden noose, and I would be foolish to not take action immediately. Why spend another year working my butt off for someone else to enjoy their toes in the water and their butt in the sand? Why spend another day paying for someone else's yacht? Why spend another day hustling for *their* Honeymoon Life? The good thing is, *"No matter how long you have traveled in the wrong direction, you can always turn around."* (Unknown)

"Fool" seems too harsh of a word, but blinded or shortsighted could fit the bill. While I was an intrapreneur at my second-to-last day job, we were "attempting" to be entrepreneurs. In the spirit of living *The Honeymoon Life*, Farhad, the boys, and I would often go dirt bike riding. This is what it says on the "Our Story" page of motovateddesigns.com:

There's no more appropriate place for an idea for a motocross-related company to be born than on the track. Farhad and Gianna Rahmani have been riding dirt bikes for fun since they got married in 2002. It naturally became a family pastime with their two boys, Nikolas and Dominik. In between working (together) at the best real estate and property management company in Maryland, school, track & field, tennis and football, "Team Rahmani" hits the dirt bike track every chance they get.

In 2016, the boys graduated to their first clutch-controlled bike. They picked it up pretty quickly and, under the canopy in between riding sessions, an excited chat among the fam about how motivated the boys were led to the idea of "MOTOvated." And talk about motivation – the logo was created, the corporate papers were filed, and the first shirt was designed in less than a week.

Team Rahmani centers around the values of faith, love, support, family time, hard work, and fun. All of the MOTOvated Designs are a reflection of these values.

MOTOvated Designs was officially in business. Six years later, it's nowhere near where a company backed by that much motivation should be.

I don't know who said it, but one of my all-time favorite quotes is *"When you state what you want, you have to start making it happen, or you have to start making excuses,"* and my least favorite thing is making excuses. No one has known that MOTOvated Designs has been a "failed" venture (based on our standards, at least), so I haven't had to tell them any excuses. But I've been telling *myself* excuses. This said, after reading all the books I've had, this doesn't scare or embarrass me at all. What has been discovered as a secret to the most successful is that you can't be afraid of failure, and that the biggest successes have come after the biggest of them. We are ready for our big success.

The mistake we made, and call it an excuse if you will, is that we rushed into this venture with only motivation and without a plan. What comes after the idea, the logo, the entity creation, and even the product? We didn't have a single system in place to sell, scale, or succeed. While my favorite type of side hustle is the monetized hobby (since day hustling™ is about doing what *you* enjoy doing), a hobby won't get you to financial freedom. A hobby is fun and casual; a hustle is fun *with intention* – it's formal, planned, thorough, careful, and it's full-time, which means you can't do it on the side. Hustling implies speediness and a *rush* towards something. How can you be free before 40 (or in time for whatever deadline you set for yourself) if you don't hustle day in and day out? Doing it casually won't get you there.

To be able to sell, scale, and succeed takes time – *full-time* – to carry out your plan of action. Unfortunately, MOTOvated Designs hasn't gotten any time or attention (let alone full-time or focus) because of my day job. Ever read *The One Thing* by

Gary Keller? I succeeded at my day job and our side "hustle" failed.

I refuse to continue being a fool, at least now that I know I've been acting like one. If I want to make money to the point of financial freedom, then I need to put all of my time and attention into my plan. And if I want to do it by the time I'm 40, I sure better hustle.

State What You Want

Up until I gave my notice to my last day job, I hadn't told anyone of my goal to retire by 40. I regret this for two reasons – one, because my leaders took steps to put me in a position to grow within the company and, two, because if I had put it out into the world when I made the goal, I would have had to start making it happen, rather than finding security in my excuses until now.

I dealt with an internal struggle throughout the tenure of my last day job. If you recall, this day job started when we relocated to Florida and Farhad retired; it was before he turned 50. The idea of joining him in retirement to do what we wanted to do by the time I turned 40 came to my head and it sounded great, but that's all it was – an idea. It wasn't written down and

I didn't have a plan nor a vision. My day job consumed most of my days (and nights) and I enjoyed it. If I couldn't see myself reaching my goal of retiring by 40, the next best thing was to keep reaching new heights in my career. As ambitious as I am, I was committed to doing the best job I could, and being promoted and earning more felt great. Thankfully, the people I worked with are true leaders – they understood and were proud of me for my decision to leave.

I can even joke that this was all their fault – they gave me writing assignments and complimented my writing skills; they held leadership classes in which they asked us to read *The One Thing* and to write out our personal mission statements; they were models in philanthropy; they were thought-leaders; they were angel investors; they gave me the opportunity to manage an extra-large region giving me the window-time to listen to audiobooks, videos, and podcasts; they treated us to events on their yachts; they taught concepts like "eat that frog;" and they didn't want our positions to be the last ones we held, but they wanted the company to be the last job we worked at. For me, they succeeded!

I wish I could say that it was my job in operations and business development that made me sensitive to deadlines, but I have always been more of a procrastinator, and I work better under pressure. You may not be able to get from that sentence whether I said something good or bad about myself, but certainly working under the pressure of time gave me the sense of urgency needed to do something as bold as retiring from my 20-year career.

Parkinson's Law surmises that *"Work expands to fill the time available for its completion."* If you give yourself 30 days to clean your home, they say, it will take you 30 days. But if you give yourself three hours, it will take three hours. As I mentioned, the idea of retiring by the time I turn 40 came to mind four years ago, so I've basically taken all four years.

Over these years, there were three instances that I wrote my goals down – apparently, that wasn't enough. As I mentioned earlier, I read books that taught me a lot of things that could help me reach my goals, but this was knowledge that I didn't put into practice. I was too comfortable with the security my day job provided us and all the time I thought I had to come up with a plan. It wasn't until I turned 39 that I started making the move. After all, I only had one year left.

A sense of urgency is a quality that has taken me far in my career. I responded immediately to teammates, prospects, and clients. Realizing that my teammates' work depended on a response from me, knowing that a prospect was not only expecting to hear from me, but from my competitors as well, or understanding that a client's concern was their only concern, it was always my priority to respond as quickly as possible. However, this sense of urgency didn't translate into reaching my own personal goal, which I had pushed aside time and time again because there was no pressure.

It's both the pressure of time and the need to impress that creates this sense of urgency. I can't seem to find the right word to describe this need, but I don't believe I'm referring to pretentiousness, narcissism, or flamboyance here, and I don't think this need is a bad thing. When I Googled "the need to wow," the top results are about how to overcome the urge to impress, how to get freedom from the need to impress, and how to stop living to impress.

I don't want undeserved credit and unearned attention. However, I feel great pride in "wowing" others, and knowing that I do only motivates me to do things faster/sooner than expected, and also to do more than, and differently than, expected. I would be dishonest to say I don't enjoy it when someone is impressed with the quality of my work or the creativity in my ideas. I would love it if you finished this book and told me *"Wow, that's a great idea, G! Well done!"*

Of course, it feels good when someone thanks me for help, especially if it was sooner or greater than expected. It's not that I expect gratitude; that's not what I help them *for*. In these cases, I'm pretty awkward in receiving the praise, so much so that I try to remain anonymous whenever possible. It's the fact that I did help someone, and there's no greater sense of fulfillment than that.

Circling back to doing things sooner than expected, I know there are always people that tell you not to send an e-mail late at night or on the weekend, but what seems like, and probably is, workaholism is less a reflection of any obsession I may have that someone is waiting for me, but more an addiction of wanting to provide them the answer or solution they are seeking as quickly as possible.

I feel great satisfaction from *being* different and from *doing* things differently than expected. For example, I can remain calm in situations in which someone else would have been stressed or be positive when someone else would be in despair. Whether someone sees riding dirt bikes as "cool" or not, it often surprises people to find that I, the "nerd" they more often associate with, ride. It amazes people that I got married at 19, less than eight months after meeting Farhad, and that we have a college freshman and a high school junior.

Nobody expected it when I dropped out of Cal or that someone like me would have tattoos (my first one actually made my mom cry – I'm sorry, Ma)! It surprises others that I've skydived before (we did it on our 10th wedding anniversary) and that we've been married for 20 years now. And it *shocked* others when we left our "golden geese."

Make It Happen

There are a few challenges that life throws our way that we would prefer not to face, but there are several challenges that I love to meet head on, including goals that I set for myself. When you put these out into the world, of course you don't want to look bad by failing. Rising up to the challenge is impressive in and of itself, but beating the challenge is more impressive. It's about proving to yourself that you can do anything and make anything happen, yes, but it certainly is motivating to do it in front of the "world." There are two schools of thought about this.

Some say that telling other people your goals and plans will attract negative energy, and I believe that this perspective comes from a place of fear – fear that people would rather see you fail and fear of failure itself. When it comes to the law of attraction, you will attract exactly these. In *The Go-Giver*, a book by Bob Burg and John D. Mann, Pindar tells Joe, *"In life, you often don't get what you want. But here's what you do get — You get what you expect. Go looking for the best in people, and you'll be amazed at how much talent, ingenuity, empathy and goodwill you'll find."*

When I see other people challenge themselves to reach a goal, let's say on social media, I'm not competing against them. While I don't see anything wrong with a little healthy competition, it's about becoming part of their journey and I root for them to win. Their winning has no ill-effect on my winning; on the contrary, it creates increased motivation. If they can do it, I can do it, and I believe that if you put your goal out into the world, you will attract cheerleaders and you will inspire them to reach their own goals. Imagine the feeling when someone tells you that you inspired them — it's amazing!

I have always struggled with maintaining a healthy weight. If I'm not on a diet and losing weight, I'm constantly eating and gaining weight. I gained 60 pounds during both of my pregnancies, and each boy was only seven pounds — I was quite plump, and it wasn't "all baby" like some other mommas, but rather all me. Thankfully, I've had a couple of aha! moments throughout the years that instilled a mindset in me to always keep trying to improve my eating habits rather than accept them as they are.

First, Farhad has an overweight cousin who once said with pride that she used to be a size two. She could have said any size that meant she was healthier than she was as she said that, but the point is that she was proud of what she was *before* without any intention of getting healthy again, and I realized that I never want to be like that. I always want to be *better* than my old self and proud of the person I'm becoming rather than who I was.

Another aha! moment for me occurred when scrolling through my LinkedIn feed one day. I was so excited about what I read that I forgot to note who said it and his or her exact words, but it impressed upon me that, if I use the mindset it takes me to be successful in one area of my life and utilized it to help me succeed in an area I'm struggling with, I can succeed at anything. This made perfect sense! If I can succeed at my day job, then I can succeed at losing weight.

And I did lose weight, though I didn't reach my ultimate goal weight right away. I had this wish to weigh what I used to when I first got my driver's license – 115 pounds, which is right in the middle of the healthy Body Mass Index (BMI) range for someone of my age, gender, and height. It wasn't until I "publicly" challenged myself that I finally reached this goal. I called it "G's Driver's License Weight Challenge," and I posted about it on my social media platforms and documented my journey to success on my blog, fwordsaremyfavorite.com (#fitness). On top of reaching my goal, it was so fulfilling to hear from people that I've inspired them to get fit!

The need to "impress" is about *putting inspiration* in someone's heart, *positively influencing* their mind, *stirring up* creativity and confidence in themselves, and *exciting* them into action. These are the synonyms for the word "impress" that I'm talking about, and I hope I've impressed upon you the importance of this need. Once I announced my retirement and told my teammates that it was to focus on our investments and on my writing, they expressed their excitement for me as well as their own desire to "one day" have the courage and ability to pursue their own dreams. The possibility that this book inspires them to follow their dreams and provides an actual bridge to *fulfill* their dreams creates an overwhelming sense of urgency – and sense of responsibility – that only confirms I made the right decision in diverting all of my time and attention to publishing this book as soon as I possibly can.

And it is sad to remember that other people's handcuffs aren't even golden. Listen to the desperation and relief in the following excerpt from *Shoe Dog: A Memoir by the Creator of Nike* by Phil Knight. *"This is – the moment,' I said. 'This is the moment we've been waiting for. Our moment. No more selling someone else's brand. No more working for someone else. Onitsuka has been holding us down for years. Their late deliveries, their mixed-up orders, their refusal to hear and implement our design ideas – who among us isn't sick of dealing with all that? It's time we faced facts: If we're going to succeed, or fail, we should do so on our own terms, with our own ideas – our own brand. Let's look at this as our liberation. Our Independence Day.'"*

Well, retiring is the first step. Getting to write is a dream for me! But the idea was flawed – being financially free by the time I'm 40 is the real goal, the real liberation, the real Independence Day. Retiring is a *step* in the plan to reach that goal. I'm putting the goal out there to you right now, with the publishing of this book – step two.

CHAPTER FIVE

THE QUESTIONS THAT ARE HOLDING YOU BACK

"The only limit to our realization of tomorrow will be our doubts of today."

Franklin D. Roosevelt

Job Security

Working for someone else isn't going to help us reach our goals fast enough or at all, but I can't quit my job! How can I? It would be irresponsible. We have bills to pay and now, of all times to decide to do this, Nikolas's first college tuition bill is due. My day job did a fine "job" in ensuring that we didn't qualify for any federal student aid. But we expected that based on our income, so we've been investing in Maryland 529 plans for both boys.

We also have mouths to feed. We went from a family of four to a family of six as soon as the boys got girlfriends. I remember Farhad and I going out to eat back in the day. Back then, it was just the two of us, and rarely did we do anything fancier than fast food. When Nikolas and Dominik came along, it was a while until we started ordering food off the menu for them, but eventually, they were big enough to eat their own kids' meals. As they grew, the kids' menu was not fulfilling them and sometimes not even one regular-sized meal was enough for each of them.

As our household income grew, I believe we did well with ensuring that our expenses didn't stay on par with it – it is important to use your new income for growing your assets and wealth instead of blowing it on everything else. Farhad is *fantastic* in the kitchen (boy, do I love a man who can cook!), so home-cooked meals were just as good, actually better, than eating out. But we enjoyed the liberty to pursue our hobbies, travel, and we did eat out more.

My day job had me eating at nice restaurants all the time. I couldn't take the boys out to Burger King after eating at Ruth's Chris. And even then, we'd go somewhere in the "middle" like Outback or Manny's Chophouse, and it wasn't until I retired that we went to Ruth's Chris or somewhere similar for an ordinary night out. And, there are often six of us now.

In addition to bellies, we have gas tanks to fill. Farhad is quite handy, so he has a truck to lug around his various tools. By the way, messing with the boys is quite fun, so I posted about Farhad being good with his hands once (he refinished our dining table, as well as built a bridge in our attic so that he could hang a pull-up bar in our home gym). I included a winky face emoji, and the boys reacted as I expected (insert *menacing laugh* here)! It's important to keep things light and fun when you have the opportunity.

Anyway, Farhad *is* quite the handyman and likes to join our contractors when working on our properties, so it's important to have a truck for buying and bringing material. We also need a truck for our "toy hauler" so we can go dirt bike riding. And we all know how gas guzzling trucks are. Thankfully, Nikolas was a strange one and put off getting his driver's license until recently, but Dominik started driving as soon as he could (like "normal" kids). On top of the huge car insurance increases, that's a lot more gas to have to pay for, and prices hit an all-time high this year and are continuing to climb.

Do you have a personal budget? Our personal budget includes the following line items:

BOYS ALLOWANCE – an amount we just more than doubled when we set our 2022 budget

BOYS COLLEGE SAVINGS

CAR & TRUCK

CAR INSURANCE

DIRT BIKE INSURANCE

STREET BIKE INSURANCE

CELL PHONES

CHARITABLE CONTRIBUTIONS

CREDIT MONITORING

DIRT BIKE RIDING

GIFTS & HOLIDAYS

GROCERIES

HAIR CUTS

HOA FEES

INTERNET

JUST MOVE – while we have a home gym, Farhad likes to use the leg machines at our local fitness center

LIFE INSURANCE

MEALS & ENTERTAINMENT

MINIMUM SAVINGS TRANSFER – we budget to put money away for emergencies; when that fund is at a certain threshold, the money goes to our investments

MORTGAGE PAYMENTS

PEACOCK TV – so we can watch Supercross and Motocross

PRIME MEMBERSHIP – we finally signed up for this in 2020; I took a fun poll and apparently, we were one of the few households that didn't have Amazon Prime before the pandemic

RING – home security

TRAVEL

UNCATEGORIZED EXPENSES (OTHER)

UTILITIES

ELECTRICITY

WATER

VITAMIN SHOPPE – we have protein shakes on auto-delivery

Your budget line items may or may not be as specific as ours, but I prefer to keep track of, and budget for, certain expenditures separately, especially if they are recurring costs. What are your budget line items?

In addition to paying our bills, my day job provides us group health insurance. Thank God we all work out and are generally healthy, but our loved ones and we have experienced, or are currently facing, our fair share of issues. You never know what can happen and it is too risky not to have coverage for unforeseen medical bills.

My day job also offered a 401k plan, though we didn't take advantage of it. When Farhad retired, we decided to roll both our plans into self-directed ROTH IRAs because he has the time to manage the funds himself. Today, we are using these funds for asset-based lending, in which we lend money to homebuilders and investors. Some of these funds (as well as non-retirement funds, as long as they're not commingled) are also invested in stocks and cryptocurrency. This said, we understand your 401k plan is a big reason why you wouldn't want to quit your day job.

I also mentioned how having certain types of debt could be good. Consumer debt is not one of these types. We pay off our credit cards every single month, we have no personal or car loans, and we paid off our student loans decades ago. We've been buying our rental properties with cash, but once Farhad fixes them up, we refinance the homes to get the equity out to put into additional properties. This technique of real estate investment is called the BRRRR method – Buy, Rehab, Rent, Refinance, Repeat. However, refinancing requires proof of income, and the easiest way is to provide your W-2s and paystubs. If we wanted to invest our money into purchasing a large franchise or an apartment building and needed a loan, then what kind of income can we show if I quit my job? We'd need to start building our credit through our businesses, which we haven't done so far, unfortunately. It was easier and quicker to do it the other way since my focus and attention have been on my day job.

Once I was "enlightened," my brain was on overdrive. It wasn't just that I didn't want to be an employee anymore; it was that being an employee was holding us back from investing more and making more of our money work for us. Farhad and I have big dreams and lots of creative ideas. And not only do we have ideas, but we also have the experience and work ethic to make these ideas work. We already "know" what it takes to be successful – we've done it. The problem? Even with this confidence, we were too scared to give up our job security. And it's not just risking my current salary. It's risking *all* that we've worked for thus far – all of the years and all that we've done and accomplished to reach our current status. And it's not only that we were secure, we were also comfortable – we provide our boys everything they need, we travel plenty, and there's nothing we're lacking. But our dreams are much bigger than just secure and comfortable. Security is important, but the problem with comfortable? It's in the comfort zone where dreams die.

My Dream Life

As I said, we already had a few solid ideas of what we wanted to pursue, but idea after idea came and they only confused Farhad and me as to which direction to head towards. My passion, as I realized throughout this process, is writing. Feeding people is Farhad's passion. And regardless of which direction we took, our vision was that we'd do it side-by-side – it's the foundation of *The Honeymoon Life*.

To analyze our ideas and options, Farhad and I reviewed all of our key takeaways from the *Rich Dad* series of books. You'll have to read these books yourself, and I highly recommend them. Robert Kiyosaki gives a more detailed and clearer explanation than I do of why you should quit your day job as soon as possible. Moreover, he doesn't just explain what his Rich Dad taught him; he tells you the specific steps you need to take.

Farhad and I needed to prioritize our ideas because those that remained on our list to pursue are ideas we believe in. We realized, however, that we can't do all of them at once. We needed to direct our focus on what will get us to our goal the fastest, and the safest. Well, how can anything be "safe" without job "security?" How can we minimize our risk? Back to the question I asked in the beginning of this chapter – how can I quit my job? In addition to all the ideas that were coming out were questions like these. Eventually, the question became the answer – simple!

Fifteen days into that 50-day whirlwind I mentioned – February 24, 2022, to be exact, and I only know this since it's documented in our text messages – the tables turned for Farhad and me. For the first time (of many times thereafter), I texted *him* a link to something, and it was an interview that Robert Kiyosaki did on Chandler Bolt's Self Publishing School podcast about how Robert sold 46 million copies of his self-published book, *Rich Dad, Poor Dad*.

After reading his books then listening to this interview, it reinforced the idea that my love of writing could be my true golden goose. The book I mentioned I started writing in 2016 is about love and relationships and what I believe will help relationships not only last longer than they are currently averaging, but be happier and more fulfilling. It has not been published because I didn't have the time to devote to complete writing it and, more importantly, to properly sell it.

The message in this book is so important for me to get out to the world, but it holds the same fate as MOTOvated Designs. I need time to focus my attention on the book, but family time comes first, and my day job took the rest of my time. A lot of that time was spent on the road and I stopped wasting all of those hours and took advantage of them. There was no more hearing at leisure and a whole lot more listening to podcasts, book summaries, and videos, including more on investing, on publishing, on e-commerce, on food businesses, on meditation, and on habits. I can't count how many more books I've read, how many videos I've watched, or how many podcasts I've listened to since this past February.

Just over a month later, *"I was on the road listening to Lewis Howes's 3/6/2022 episode of The School of Greatness. More often than not, my mind wanders as I listen to any video, podcast, or audiobook causing me to continuously rewind, and such was the case today. I kept thinking about how we can continue to have the benefits of my job (salary, health insurance, and proof of income) while working on our own business.*

This thought led to the following wish — why can't someone pay me a salary to grow my business instead of theirs?

"And, just like that, the idea of Day Hustle™ was born, though the name came later on in the drive. Referring back to the idea that if I want something, I must give it away first, I thought about starting a business where I paid my employees their current salary, and their job would be to build their business. Their business profits would be our income until they grew it to a point where they, themselves, could retire. At that moment, Lewis's podcast recaptured my attention as his guest, John Assaraf, said, '…I built my companies by training my employees not on the skills that they needed, but on how spectacular they were as human beings, and that greatness was within them.'

"There are no rules in business, and it couldn't have been a timelier message from God, affirmation, or sign that I was on to something. The thought of quitting my day job had Farhad and me pushing to figure out which business idea we should pursue and when to pursue it (and I was starting to have too many ideas, which was causing confusion). We didn't want to put too many eggs in one basket, but which basket will get us to the point where we feel comfortable with me leaving my day job? Through Day Hustle™, we would be investing in multiple 'employees' and paying them a salary felt much more appealing than paying large lump sums to buy traditional businesses or franchises, which was what we were leaning towards.

"More and more reasons why this was a great idea were flying in my head, and I had to get it all out so I could process them and see how it would actually work. As soon as I was able, I pulled out a pen and a notepad and wrote everything about the Day Hustle™ idea down.

"I couldn't wait to tell Farhad all about it. As usual, Farhad and I were on the phone multiple times over my drive. It killed me to hold everything in, but I knew I couldn't tell him over the phone. My ETA at home would have been just after he would leave to pick something up that he bought for Dominik. The location was a half hour detour for me, but it was still better than Farhad going all the way there, so I continued to hold my tongue. I couldn't hold my thoughts, though, and they kept repeating that 'we are going to be financially free soon.'

"By the time I eventually got home, Farhad was heading to one of our properties. I ate a quick lunch as I transferred my Day Hustle™ notes onto my laptop and ran a few numbers. I'd need Farhad to help me work them out later, but the ROI that I was estimating was only getting me more and more excited. We planned to pick Nikolas up from school at two to go play tennis together (Dominik had baseball practice). As soon as we were courtside, I told Farhad we were going to be financially free very soon. He nodded his head, seemingly taking it as a simple affirmation because of all of the reading, planning, and brainstorming of the past two months. I clarified and let it all out."

On April 1, 2022, I decided to start a daily journal. I knew everything was changing and it was changing fast and for the better. I wanted to document it to enjoy the moments and to document it in the hopes that it could someday help someone in his or her journey. I started with the day before, **March 31, 2022**, when the idea of Day Hustle™ was born, and the recap above was my first journal entry. (Did you guess correctly?)

The following are highlights of the subsequent journal entries as they relate to our journey from wanting to publish my book on love and relationships, to the plan of publishing this one (clearly a different book than the one I had started in 2016), to my retirement:

April 1 – Farhad and I wrote down our vision together. We updated and reviewed our financial statements and determined how much more our investments had to make in order for us to be financially free.

April 3 – Farhad and I continued working on "prioritizing" our ideas to see which business(es) to pursue first or at all. We considered the cost to start each endeavor, the type of actions required to run the business, the estimated time to making profit, and the scalability, among other various points we learned from Robert Kiyosaki's books. This had me thinking how writing could fit into the plan – there's no cost to writing until I'm ready to get it edited, designed, and published, but where would it go from there? I still also had the major concern of how to get the book into as many hands as possible.

April 4 – On an early morning drive, I was thinking of the Day Hustle™ idea. I thought it would solve a big problem for the many people that need to quit their day jobs but can't (or won't). Perhaps, if I wrote a book about this new opportunity for them, many more people would get to know us and, in turn, be more apt to buy my book on love and relationships. I decided then to write a book on Day Hustle™ first.

April 14 – Farhad and I celebrated our 20ᵗʰ wedding anniversary.

April 18 – After interviewing a few attorneys, Farhad and I chose to meet with Jared Mangum of Forward Law who confirmed our Day Hustle™ idea was legal.

April 20 – I was wishing I had an angel employer™ myself because I had little time to work on the Day Hustle™ idea due to my day job. (Make sure you develop your hustle on your own time with your own equipment and assets, since you could potentially lose some ownership rights to your intellectual property. When I was developing mine, I was very careful to do so on my own time, and on my own equipment. Also, you should be careful not to violate any non-compete or non-solicitation provisions you may have with your employer.)

April 21 – I started writing this book! I wrote a whopping two sentences before my day job interrupted me.

April 24 – Farhad and I decided that I would be the first day hustler™ so that I could have time to devote to my writing. I would quit my day job, and we'd only need a portion of the proceeds from the sale of the current property we were flipping to get the Day Hustle™ company started. But I would wait until May 23rd, when the sale was scheduled to close, to give my notice.

April 30 – I woke up and thought about how many books I'd like to sell, since I needed to make a goal. This part of *Think and Grow Rich* was difficult for me because living *The Honeymoon Life* isn't only about being rich. But I have seen book covers that say, "A Million Copies Sold," and when I put it in terms of how many people I can help – how many lives I can impact – I gained some clarity as to how to set this goal.

I calculated what selling a million books would mean. If we get 70% royalty from Amazon at the price of $9.99, that would be $6.99 per book less delivery costs, and just shy of $7M if we sold a million books. I wanted to see if this was realistic – *attainable* in SMART goals – and remembered the stats that I had added in Chapter One, as well as those from Side Hustle Nation's survey. If there are an estimated 70M Americans with side hustles, 1M of that is 1.4%. With the increasing number of side hustlers, this percentage is less. And with the side hustlers throughout the entire world, this percentage could be infinitesimal. If we target side hustlers well, then I think this is attainable. I would need to determine the cost at which the book would be sold, as well as the timeframe in which I'd like to sell this many.

May 6 – Farhad asked me what I wanted for Mother's Day, and I took the opportunity to ask him if I could give my notice sooner than the 23rd. I am uncomfortable working without telling my employer that my plans have changed and I want to tell him as soon as possible. My job is also remote, so I don't get many chances to see him in person, and I will not give my notice any other way. Next week, I'd have an opportunity as I was driving down for a team meeting. Farhad agreed to give me what feels like the best Mother's Day gift ever, next to our boys, of course.

May 11 – I announced my upcoming retirement to my employer.

June 3rd – Farhad and I went to turn in all of the work stuff I had at home, and we had a team lunch to celebrate my last day on the job. Even on my last day, I worked beyond closing hours and wrapped everything up that evening.

Losing all of the benefits that a day job provides would be terrifying – for most people, it would be paralyzing. You can even say that successful workers are *addicted* to the security and even the success they have at their day jobs. However, they can be even more successful when growing their own businesses and pursuing their dreams. With Day Hustle™, *"Don't quit your day dream,"* like Sara Blakely of Spanx says, but do yourself a favor – take action and *do* quit your day job!

Chapter Six

Day Hustle™ Explained – The Answer to Your Questions

"The only impossible journey is the one you never begin." Tony Robbins

I f you're like most people, then you've read and responded to several job ads and job descriptions throughout your lifetime. Here is Day Hustle™'s:

JOB TITLE: Day Hustler™

DIRECT SUPERVISOR: Yourself

PURPOSE: To grow your side hustle

TYPE: Full-time

SALARY: Your current salary

LOCATION: Wherever you want

SCHEDULE: Whenever you want

RESPONSIBILITIES: Whatever you want

BENEFITS: Health insurance, access to other group coverage, 401k retirement plan

Simple enough? I think so. But the skills and qualifications required to be a successful day hustler™ will take a bit more to describe, and we'll discuss them in the following chapter. There are also a bit more benefits to discuss than those listed. As I mentioned earlier, the Day Hustle™ idea will be mutually beneficial. Let's start with these benefits.

Where to Find the Numbers

My journey to retirement was accelerated due to audiobooks I listened to, so I wrote this book in a way to allow you to listen to it. Though it may be difficult to picture the numbers, I will explain how they work. It is also important for you to see the numbers, so you can request access to the scale and calculations that I've put into tables by going to dayhustlers.com.

How It Works

Day Hustle™ will pay your salary and provide benefits until you grow your business large enough to retire from Day Hustle™. As a day hustler™, you will also own 49% of the company and Day Hustle™ will temporarily own the remaining 51%. Day Hustle™ will determine if profits are needed to grow the company, or if distributions can be made to the owners. When growth of the business and when the tax code allows, Day Hustle™ will take all the profits from the business to pay it back for the amount it is paying, and has paid out, in salary. Once Day Hustle™ has recouped its original investment in you, plus the profit listed on the scale, you can buy out Day Hustle™ and you will be 100% owner of your company. And here is some good news! You do not have to pay any cash out of pocket to buy Day Hustle™'s interest. The purchase price is simply 3% of gross revenue paid out over 10 years.

This is exciting because the faster you build your company, the faster you are 100% owner, plus we pay you your salary to do it. It is all up to you! It may sound daunting, but the amount of time it will take for you to be able to retire all depends on how profitable you build your company. It could be as short as 18 months or even *less!* Does retiring in the next year and a half sound good to you? Moreover, your business income will increase as you build, and once Day Hustle™ is bought out, you determine when and how much to take in distributions! Does making 7.5 times your salary sound good to you? If so, keep reading!

Here are target scenarios for how the numbers will work. Again, you can follow along by requesting access to the tables at dayhustlers.com. I'll use three examples – if you are currently making $50k a year, $100k a year, or $150k a year at your day job.

EXAMPLE ONE:

Let's start with $50k a year, and let's say your side hustle income currently equals 20% of that amount, which is $10k a year, for a total of $60k income. This means that Day Hustle™

will pay you a gross monthly salary of \$4,166.67 and your monthly business profits of \$833.33 will go to Day Hustle™. Day Hustle™ is losing \$3,333.33 at month one. According to Side Hustle Nation's survey, the average side hustler spends, at most, 16 hours per *week* on their business. Eight hours is 33% of a day you are now devoting to your business, so 40 more hours a week would mean 350% more time. But even with all that additional time and attention, let's be conservative and say you grow your monthly profits by only 10% each month. This means that at month two, your monthly profits have increased to \$1,250.

At month two, Day Hustle™ pays you \$4,166.67 in salary, but it only loses \$2,916.67. At the same rate of growth each month, your monthly profits will be \$2,083.33 at month four, which equals 50% of your monthly salary, and Day Hustle™ loses the same amount. At month nine, your monthly profits will equal your monthly salary. This is the point where the amount being paid to Day Hustle™ and the amount Day Hustle™ pays out breaks even.

If your business profits start at an amount equal to 20% of your salary, Day Hustle™ has determined that its profit after being repaid the salary will be 50% of the amount it has paid out. But remember, you are making at least what you did at your day job while building ownership in your company. This payment to Day Hustle™ is not out of your pocket, but out of the company profits.

So, to pay you a gross annual salary of $50k, Day Hustle™'s goal is to make $25k a year. Assuming you continue to grow at 10% per month, a month after the breakeven point, month 10, your monthly profits will be $4,583.33. With still paying you your salary, Day Hustle™ is finally recouping its investment starting with $416.67. At month 14, your profits have reached the $75k mark. At month 17, your profits have reached $90k and Day Hustle™ has fully recouped its investment. After a year and a half of day hustling™, you will have increased your profits by 900%! After our profits of $25k, your income is now $65k all in business profits instead of $60k, with $50k of it as ordinary earned income and only $10k from profits. You also own your own business, and it is growing.

At this point, it's time for you to buy out Day Hustle™, retire as an employee of Day Hustle™, and retire from working for anyone but yourself! You continue to work how you want, where you want, and when you want. Without a day job, you have the time and focus to grow your business. We were conservative and estimated growth of 10% a month, but there's no limit to your potential. Think of how much you will have learned about your business in the 18 months of focusing on it. You will have perfected your craft and you can further increase your business profits to $100k, $500k, or even $1M+ a year! There are countless startups that began as side hustles that exploded and went public. You can become a millionaire, a billionaire, or whatever your goal is. Whatever it is, you'll be financially free, and Day Hustle™'s annual profit amount stays the same.

EXAMPLE TWO:

Let's move on to the next example – if your salary is $100k a year. We'll use the same variables for current profits at 20%, 10% growth, and Day Hustle™ profit at 50%. It's amazing how the math works, but the breakeven point remains month nine and you are retired by month 18. Only in this scenario, your profits will have grown from $20k to $180k!

EXAMPLE THREE:

At a salary of $150k a year and the same variables as the first two examples, your profits will grow from $30k to $270k! Again, these tables are all laid out for you, and access can be requested at dayhustlers.com.

Also note that, if you start at a higher profits percentage, the annual profit Day Hustle™ will receive is less. The tables you can access show how the Day Hustle™ profit could scale down to 15%. Similarly, if you grow your profits at a faster rate than 10% a month, you'll not only be retiring sooner, but we provide incentives for a faster buyout.

The tables outlined vary from retirement in 18 months to more aggressive timeframes for retirement at 12 months and even four months. Once everything began to click for me – once I knew being an employee is not the way to financial freedom, and once I realized that all I needed was the time to focus on my own goals – it took just shy of four months until I retired from my property/community management career and, if I can do it, then you can do it!

For you, however, there's little risk because Day Hustle™ is investing in *you*. If you didn't make the connection, I am the original day hustler™, and my purpose is to grow Honeymoon Media. But Farhad and I funded Day Hustle™ with our *own* money so I was truly on my own and "retired" when I quit my day job. I had 100% of the profits, but also 100% of the risk.

I am taking the risk, in part, because I want to fund many more people like you and accelerate the success of many more businesses. From book sale profits alone, Honeymoon Media could be reverting an amount to Day Hustle™ that would cover about 50 to *150* new day hustlers™, and this is only using the examples of $50k to $150k annual salaries. It is also only taking into account the initial funding, not the return of and on investments that we plan on re-investing into more day hustlers™. Moreover, we did it this way to prove that angel employment™ works, and the proof is in the pudding.

If you were wondering if Day Hustle™ is available to you even if you haven't started your side hustle or if your current business profits are less than 20%, the answer is yes. You'll go through the same evaluation process outlined in Chapter Eight, but your application, idea, interview, and plan need to be compelling. Once I became a day hustler™, Honeymoon Media didn't have *any* income to pay back Day Hustle™ and it won't have any until this book sells. But the angel employment™ concept is something we believe the world desperately needs right now, and Farhad and I were compelled to invest in it.

Now, let's quickly discuss the tax issue we mentioned in Chapter Three. Setting up your company as an S-corp after you buy out Day Hustle™ can solve most of the self-employment tax issues. I urge you to read Robert Kiyosaki's books and speak to your CPA, and it will be pretty clear how your taxes will take care of themselves when you are generating this much more income from your own business.

What Makes It Possible

It is 100% possible for you to retire from Day Hustle™ in four, 12, or 18 months because the Day Hustle™ system provides the **pressure** of time. Grant Cardone went from broke to millionaire in 90 days, as he discussed in his interview with Lewis Howes on *The School of Greatness*.

Farhad's been updating our bathrooms recently and a practical analogy came to mind when he replaced our showerhead with one that is wide and multi-functional. At the widest setting, the showerhead provides a nice, relaxed, mist-like sprinkle. But at the narrowest setting, when the water is concentrated to the center of the showerhead, it provides a high-pressure, jet-like spray. It takes a fraction of the time to get all that shampoo out of my hair using the latter setting rather than the former.

The Day Hustle™ system also brings you close enough to the edge of security and to the point of no return that you force yourself to be 100% all-in. If you don't perform and grow your business according to the agreement we enter, you risk a higher

Day Hustle™ profit percentage or termination. Believe me, this **accountability** is not to worry you or stress you out. On the contrary, it is **motivation**. *"Without a sense of urgency, desire loses its value,"* Jim Rohn once said.

As I described in Chapter Four, the pressure of time and the **need to impress** creates the **sense of urgency** needed to get things done as soon as possible, and even faster than you set out for. If you are selected as a day hustler™, then our partnership will be announced via press release, and everyone will be rooting for your forthcoming retirement from Day Hustle™ – you're going to rise to the **challenge**, compete with yourself, and start making things happen at that point.

You will become part of a **network** of day hustlers™ that will be cheering you on and can provide resources and connections that can further propel your success – it doesn't have to be lonely at the top. Day Hustle™ already has a legal and accounting team familiar with angel employment™, as it worked with me to get to this point, and who are experts in working with entrepreneurs to help you with anything from entity creation and asset protection to bookkeeping and tax planning. We will hold day hustler™ team meetings to celebrate each other's wins and so that you can offer your products/services to each other. *The Almanack of Naval*

Ravikant by Eric Jorgenson talks about compound relationships, and Jim Rohn is often credited to have once said, *"Your network is your net worth!"*

Day Hustle™ not only provides you with the pressure of time, but it provides you with **time** itself. It will provide you the benefit of time to **focus** on your side hustle. In the book *Eat That Frog*, Brian Tracy quotes William Mathews – *"The first law of success is concentration – to bend all the energies to one point, and to go directly to that point, looking neither to the right nor the left."* While some people can choose to take the leap without Day Hustle™, the fear and uncertainty that they will inevitably face is distracting. One could argue that taking the leap in this way is the reason he or she is successful, but we'll never know the degree of size and speed his or her business could have grown without the distractions of fear and uncertainty.

If you can change one thing and alter the trajectory of your life and business, then you can apply this idea and multiply it, and the 40+ hours a week that you've been devoting to your day job can now be concentrated on your business. According to Side Hustle Nation's survey, the two biggest challenges facing side hustlers is growing their business and dealing with limited time. If time is money, tip the scales in your favor by having the time to scale your business up rapidly. Now, imagine the trajectory of how much bigger and how much faster your business will grow with all of that focused time, energy, and attention!

Day Hustle™ can also give you true life balance. When I gave my notice to my day job, one of the owners told me that he thought I could do both – keep working for the company and pursue my writing. But that's not taking into account the time I want to have with my family or anything else. One of the many qualities I admired in this same person was his devotion to his family and his freedom to put family first – with grown kids that have left the nest, he had excused himself from some work functions to hop on his weekly family Zoom call, an awesome routine to have.

I was all-in at my day job and my family, yes, but my writing was left as an afterthought. With everything you have to do to grow a successful business, imagine doing it all after working an 8- to 10- hour day (I know they are oftentimes longer). They call this the 7:00 pm to 2:00 am strategy, which encourages you to work your 9-to-5, then work another seven hours on top of it. What *type* of energy are you exerting in your second "shift?" How much time is left for your family? For you?

With the security and comfort that I had from my day job, working even more on a side hustle and sacrificing time with my family did not seem worth it. When I heard that it "just" takes five to 10 years of focus and sacrifice, with the intent of making that length of time seem like it was short, I felt like I would rather ride my day job for as long as possible. Five to 10 years of zero life balance was not fast enough – personally, I feel like we should have zero tolerance for sacrificing family time. This said, my day job itself required some sacrifices. While Farhad and I chaperoned almost all of the boys' school trips, watched almost all of their games and/or sporting events, while we rode and worked out together as much as we could, and while we're probably one of the most active families you'll ever see – while we may have been physically present – work certainly caused interruptions. Trips, vacations, and holidays often required stepping away to take urgent calls, constantly monitoring emails, sales presentations on the way to the airport, and submitting proposals in time for New Year's Eve deadlines.

For a while, I accepted that these were worth it. However, in *Wise as Fu*k,* Gary John Bishop says *"Never allow yourself to settle for 'feeling better' about a life that doesn't work. That's called stagnation and, as clichéd as it might sound, you actually are better than that."* But imagine the difference in the pie chart of your daily activities if your day job was removed. In addition to your business, in which areas of your life could you use an additional 8+ hours of attention – family time, pastimes, exercise, self-care, or sleep? Many side hustlers have reported mental breakdowns from the stress of growing their businesses while working full-time day jobs. It's because they don't have time to take care of themselves. Here's what a typical "working" day looks like for me as a day hustler™:

7:00 am wake up and write

9:00 am breakfast with Farhad (and the boys, if they're up and/or home)

10:00 am book sales and marketing activities

1:00 pm lunch with Farhad (and the boys, if they're home)

2:00 pm admin work for our businesses and investments, bookkeeping, emails

4:00 pm exercise, listening/learning

5:30 pm housework, dinner with Farhad and the boys, family time

10:00 pm social media

11:00 pm sleep

As I mentioned earlier, my last day job taught me a lot, and they are the best at systems, including those for communication, collaboration, and prioritization. On top of the above daily activities, Farhad and I apply as much as we can of what I learned from them and also have weekly *huddles*, in which we discuss our *Top Five* priorities for the week. We also have *side-by-sides (SBS or SxS)*, but Farhad and I get to do it a lot more often as we literally work side-by-side. These systems play a big part of our planning and strategizing.

You will notice that the first thing I do when I wake up is write. My morning routine has changed several times over the years to set me up for success in whatever stage of life I'm in. Nowadays, waking up to write is a personal choice and is what works for me. In my quest to be free from alarm clocks, it's ironic that I've found something that wakes me up naturally – I can't wait to get to writing and am often up way before the sun rises, especially if I was able to get to bed earlier the night before. I love it that much and can only hope that you and others find the type of passion that has you hopping out of bed, that has you coming up with new ideas at every turn, and that has you constantly wanting to talk about it.

But I would also like to give the time to **sleep** extra attention. Personally, I have a condition called hypersomnia, which means that even if I get a good night's sleep, I still get sleepy throughout the day. If you are always tired or sleepy, then I encourage you to watch an old video of mine in which I talk about hypersomnia and that I've transferred to the Day Hustle™ YouTube channel. (Beware – I cringe at how amateur this video is, but I decided not to redo it as one day, I'd like to see how far I've come.)

Anyway, while I give myself a solid eight hours of sleep at night, I often also take a nap after breakfast and/or after lunch. This said, you probably don't have hypersomnia. Most people have the opposite – *insomnia* – and I hope you are able to find ways to get a good night's sleep. Having enough sleep helps you function at peak performance, so it's not only more time that you can now devote to your business, but it's higher "quality" time – you'll be more effective, make better decisions, and reduce the amount of time you have to pay for wrong decisions. It is another powerful benefit of day hustling™.

CHAPTER SEVEN

THE QUALITIES THAT MAKE SUCCESSFUL DAY HUSTLERS™

"If you want to achieve excellence, you can get there today. As of this second, quit doing less-than-excellent work." Thomas J. Watson

I f it's not personal, then it's not business. Read that again. Day Hustle[TM] may not have any customers to service or sell products to, but it's very much about people. We want to help people like you who have the same struggles and fears we had. Angel investors are amazing as they help with business expenses. As angel employers[TM], we want to help take care of your *personal* expenses.

Who Am I?

One of the many things I learned from my last day job is that people come first. It's all about you and the qualities that make you destined for greatness, as well as knowing where you can improve. My last day job used The Predictive Index® (PI) to evaluate candidates and use a scientific approach to selection and training. It's amazingly spot on, and Day Hustle[TM] may be using it as part of its evaluation process. I thought it would be interesting to share the results of my own Behavioral Assessment. I also thought it would be important for you to know who I am, especially if you want to partner with me and with Day Hustle[TM].

Gianna will most strongly express the following behaviors:

♦ *Proactivity, assertiveness, and sense of urgency in driving to reach her goals. Openly challenges the world around her.*

♦ *Independent in putting forth her own ideas, which are often innovative and, if implemented, cause change. Resourcefully works through or around anything blocking completion of what she wants to accomplish; aggressive when challenged.*

♦ *Impatient for results, she puts pressure on herself and others for rapid implementation, and is far less productive when doing routine work.*

♦ *Task-focused; she quickly notices and pushes to fix technical problems, assertively cutting through any personal/emotional issues. Has aptitude to spot trends in data or figure out how complex systems work.*

♦ *Independent, analytical, critical, and creative thinking and action; little need for external validation before action. Private.*

♦ *Authoritative and direct, she's driven to accomplish her personal goals; she pushes through roadblocks assertively. Communication is direct, to the point, and sometimes brusque.*

Summary

Gianna is an intense, results-oriented, self-starter whose drive and sense of urgency are tempered and disciplined by her concern for the accuracy and quality of her work. Her approach to anything she does or is responsible for will be carefully thought-out, based on thorough analysis and detailed knowledge of all pertinent facts.

Strongly technically-oriented, she has confidence in her professional knowledge and ability to get things done quickly and correctly. With experience, she will develop a high level of expertise in her work and will be very aware of mistakes made either by herself or anybody doing work under her supervision. Gianna takes her work and responsibilities very seriously and expects others to do the same.

In social matters, Gianna is reserved and private, with little interest in small talk. Her interest and her energy will be focused primarily on her work, and in general she is more comfortable and open in the work environment than she is in purely social situations. In expressing herself in her work environment she is factual, direct, and authoritative.

Imaginative and venturesome, Gianna is a creative person, capable of developing new ideas, systems, plans or technology, or of analyzing and improving old ones. She relies primarily on her own knowledge and thinking, with little reference to others, to get things done. She sets a high, exacting standard for herself, and generally finds that others do not meet that standard. To earn her trust, someone must consistently meet that standard and get results; if they can do that, Gianna will do whatever she can to work with them whenever she needs to collaborate.

While she may be perceived by other people as aloof, she will earn their respect for her knowledge of her work and the soundness of her decisions.

When reviewing my own PI, it's pretty clear that I will "make things happen," but the following words and phrases stood out for me: assertiveness, aggressive, impatient, cutting through any personal/emotional issues, authoritative, direct, brusque, with little reference to others, and aloof. These stood out for me because I believe in first impressions, but I also believe in challenging the norm and redefining traditional conventions. By themselves, or depending on whom the words are describing, these words may typically give off a negative connotation. However, they can be applied in a positive way.

Interestingly, I take the sum of these words, when taken into the context of my behavioral assessment, to equal the word "fierce," another word that may sound negative like a cruel or violent animal, but can be taken as a positive quality when describing an ambitious person. Heck, even "ambitious" can be taken both ways. Upon researching the word "fierce," I came across a couple of blog articles that make it a *fierce* contender as one of my new favorite F words.

Fierce Productions, an event production company, provides the "modern" definition of the word "fierce" in its article, *Fierce Defined*. *"The modern definition of fierce is about being bold, and unapologetic in the way you choose to express yourself. It is more like a mother deer standing down a tiger, than the tiger itself. Being fierce usually means doing something that is against the norm. You might expect to face criticism for your choices from those who usually conform, but you choose to do it anyway because it brings you joy. The most obvious examples of this are pop stars like Beyoncé, whose bold, unique style often flies in the face of convention. However, anyone can be fierce, just follow your passion and don't let anyone tell you to conform."*

In her *Falling Down the Book Hole* blog, Ashley compiles several interpretations of the word "fierce." She cites *Ready Publication* when providing a definition: *"Being fierce means standing your ground when the going gets tough. [Someone] who is fierce is always looking to better [themselves] and the world around [them]."*

A big decision I had to make when writing this book was what name I should publish it under. As I listed before, many authors use their initials as pen names. In addition to the reasons that I gave earlier, many people do call me G. I have several other nicknames from family and friends, and what I love the most is when people feel comfortable enough to refer to me in these endearing and more informal ways – it means

I've done well in building a connection and making *them* feel comfortable. This said, while my research indicated that it would *not* be a good idea to use my initials as a non-fiction writer, going against the norm in this way was a "challenge" I thought would be fun to take on.

The PI helps identify a person's natural wiring, but it also helps whoever uses it to identify areas one can improve or where one needs to exert more energy. While I am considered successful, compassionate, and a team player by my peers, both personal and professional, it's because I "temper and discipline" myself in the appropriate situations. It doesn't necessarily mean that I have to change who I am, but I work hard at balancing my drive to get things done quickly and my expectations for excellence with my approach in working and communicating with others. I'm an introvert, but that doesn't mean I don't work hard at improving my skills in small talk, put extra energy into social and networking events, and I even enjoy public speaking (as long as I'm thoroughly prepared).

Who Are You?

While I remain a work in progress, a lot of the qualities noted in my personal Behavioral Assessment were those I noted when creating the Day Hustler™ Success Formula, which I did without reviewing my report for quite some time – I created the Day Hustler[TM] Success Formula as an exercise to determine if *I* have what it takes to succeed as an entrepreneur on my own.

I wouldn't feel worthy to ask you to personify certain qualities if I didn't do so myself. As you read, I've always held myself to the strictest of standards before expecting them from others. This said, the right candidates for the day hustler[TM] position will possess certain skills and qualifications, but similar to John Assaraf's approach, this is less about the skills you need to do your job – we'll let you *"mind your own business,"* as Robert Kiyosaki teaches. However, we've added the qualifications for greatness in the Day Hustler[TM] Success Formula:

Success = (pressure + accountability + motivation + need to impress + sense of urgency + challenge + network + time + focus + sleep) * (clarity + courage + faith + gratefulness + confidence + ego + positive attitude + decisiveness + obsession + stubbornness + creativity + integrity + humility + work ethic + pride + love)

Yes, it's a long equation! But while some may try to simplify it, understand that it takes A LOT to be successful, and Day Hustle[TM] is meant to help you succeed. But not to worry – you may notice that Day Hustle[TM] provides the first grouping of benefits, as discussed in the previous chapter. Multiplied by the second grouping of qualities, the "soft skills" if you will, you've got the formula for success.

First, as I mentioned in Chapter Four, it's not enough to know what your goals are, nor is it even enough to write them down – you need a clear vision and a plan to reach those goals. I believe that having **clarity** regarding what you want to achieve and what you need to do to achieve it, why you're doing it, where you want to take it, and how you're going to influence and impact this world we live in, is one of the most important ingredients for happiness and fulfillment. Not knowing what legacy you will be leaving or what legacy you want to leave behind creates fear and uncertainty, but being clear about your purpose in life and how to fulfill it is the foundation for everything else that comes afterwards.

While there are qualities you can develop and skills you can learn, fear often paralyzes even the most motivated and knowledgeable of people. Understandably so, as we discussed in Chapter Five, you may be afraid of losing the benefits of your day job. It's a reasonable fear, and though I wish I was qualified enough to provide philosophical ways of conquering fear, I'm glad Day Hustle™ *eliminates* what you need to be afraid of in the first place – you will have all of the benefits of your day job. It's an incredible life hack for job – *life* – security. Your day hustle[TM] becomes your primary source of income more secure than any day job because, by the end, you work for you. This said, Day Hustle[TM] and retirement is only a step in your plan to achieve financial freedom. Success goes beyond job security, so you will definitely need **courage** and **faith** to navigate through the unimaginable possibilities on your road to success. This is also where **gratefulness** comes in because if you recognize all of the blessings that God, or the Universe, has given you thus far, your courage and faith are magnified. I love what David Bayer said in his *Mind Hack* program that Farhad and I did together a couple of years ago – think of all of the tiny miracles that got you to where you are today!

I believe in God, and I believe in myself. In order to succeed, you also need **confidence** in yourself. You don't have to be conceited or arrogant, but you need a healthy **ego** and a **positive attitude** that you can and will do whatever it takes to succeed, that things happen for a reason – a good reason – and that they will all work out, especially if you put in the work. Once you've **decided** what you want to do and what you want to achieve, you need to be **obsessed** with succeeding. I suggest reading *Think and Grow Rich* to learn more about burning desires. Napoleon Hill says that *"When your desires are strong* *enough, you will appear to possess superhuman powers to achieve."* And if you caught Adam Sandler's new movie, *Hustle*, you would have heard his character say, *"Obsession is gonna beat talent every time."*

You need to be **stubborn** and not tolerate any other outcome than success. You have to be **creative** when things don't go your way and you need to find other ways to reach your goals. You need to eliminate excuses and make things happen, whatever it takes. Equally, if not more, important when you have this drive is that you need to have **integrity**, **humility**, the proper **work ethic**, and **pride** in what you do to always do what's right, to quickly admit when you mess up and focus on making it right, to do your work in the best and most effective way, and to continue learning and improving. You need to **love** to win, you need to love the process, you need to love working with people, and you need to love the hustle. With these qualities, you will be unstoppable – a force to be reckoned with!

One of the many things I learned from my last day job is that people come first. Elon Musk once said, *"My biggest mistake is probably weighing too much on someone's talent and not someone's personality. I think it matters whether someone has a good heart."* It's all about you – the qualities that make you, YOU!

CHAPTER EIGHT

THE STEPS TO BECOME A DAY HUSTLER™

"You miss 100% of the shots you don't take." Wayne Gretzky

I believe it usually does take money to make money, but it doesn't have to be a lot, and it doesn't have to be yours. Startups have various resources to get going, including various stages of seed funding like bootstrapping (your own money), but they also include debt funding, incubators, accelerators, angel investors, angel syndicates, crowdfunding, and venture capitalists. If these are the "seeds," then Day Hustle™, as your angel employer™, provides the soil (time), the sun (salary), and the rain (benefits) to help you and your business grow to unimaginable heights. Now, let's make it rain!

The Application Process

It's as simple as one-two-three. If you believe you have what it takes to be a day hustler™, then here are the three steps you need to take:

1. Read and understand this book.
2. Watch the explainer video on the Day Hustle™ YouTube channel.
3. Complete the application at dayhustlers.com.

You may be asked for proof of your book purchase and, if you are prompted, then note this verification code:

DELIVERLOVE. The explainer video provides a different code, and you agree to a non-disclosure of any and all information you access regarding Day Hustle™.

You can only imagine the number of people vying for the opportunity that Day Hustle™ is offering. Seriously, what wouldn't you give for the chance to get paid to do your own thing on your own terms? What wouldn't you give to increase your business profits by 900% in 18 months or less? So, in an effort to manage the amount of applications, there is a fee. If you are **confident** enough in yourself and your side hustle, you will be willing to "risk" this cost but, if you are selected as a day hustler™, then it will be reimbursed to you on your final paycheck at your retirement from Day Hustle™ and we'll be more than happy to do so.

If you don't get hired, then we'll keep your application for future consideration, and at the minimum, you would have gained clarity over the questions posed in this book. Applications will be reviewed in the order they are received and spots are limited so, if you want to be your own boss and achieve financial freedom sooner rather than later, then you need to *hustle* and take action immediately.

The Evaluation Process

Once you submit your application, the evaluation process will begin. Just like when you apply for a job, you may be asked to submit some additional documentation, but you can expect additional documents to be requested, including but not limited to:

- Resume
- Personal and professional references
- Driver's license
- Social security card
- Last three months of paystubs
- W-2s and 1099s
- Last three years of tax returns
- Last three years of personal and business financial statements
- Budget for personal expenses

In addition, you can expect similar and additional evaluation steps, including, but not limited to:

- Interview(s)
- Credit and background checks
- Behavioral assessment

- Business and market review and analysis
- Drug test

Learning to present your business for a market review and analysis is important for raising capital and pitching to investors, so it will be good practice for you. We also ask you to kindly check off this 10-step action list:

- Rate and review this book on the platform from which you purchased it (i.e. Amazon and Barnes & Noble)

- Tell your friends and family members about this opportunity (the more books we sell, the more people we can help; on the application, we'll be asking how you heard about Day Hustle™)

- Follow @dayhustleofficial, @activeretirement, and @gmrahmaniofficial on Instagram (get to know my family and me on a personal level, as well as keep up with our businesses and investments)

- Connect with me on LinkedIn (G. M. Rahmani, Entrepreneur, Investor)

- Subscribe to the *F Words Are My Favorite* blog on fwordsaremyfavorite.com (I will delve deeper into some of the finance topics I introduced in this book)

- Subscribe to the Day Hustle™ channel on YouTube (perhaps you and your business will be featured one day soon)
- Like and/or comment on the explainer video
- Sign up for e-mail and/or text alerts (for application deadlines, upcoming events, updates, giveaways, and promotions) at dayhustlers.com
- Post a pic of you while reading this book (or listening to it) on Instagram, LinkedIn, and/or Facebook, use the hashtag #dayhustlebook, and tag me and/or Day Hustle™
- Please note that the exclusive Day Hustle™ group on Facebook is private and is by invitation only; request an invitation at dayhustlers.com to gain access to VIP opportunities.

CHAPTER NINE

RESOURCES TO HELP YOU CONQUER FEAR

"Some books leave us free and
some books make us free."

Ralph Waldo Emerson

Read

A person is a sum of their experiences – it's why I've often said, though I'm sure I'm not the first, that the one thing we all have in common is that we're all different from each other. Even people who consider themselves the same as those in their "group" are different because whatever "common" principle(s) they share is/are heard and understood based on different experiences. No two people have experienced the same exact life and every difference affects how one person perceives and interprets information from the other. It's why we can't judge others and why we should always deliver love.

It's also why I've learned to love reading. Learning through books is an important part of being prepared, which helps with overcoming fear. Reading gives us the opportunity to experience other people's experiences without having personally experienced them. Similarly, we can learn so much quicker by reading a book, with information that took years for the author to learn himself/herself.

It's why you read books and think you've heard the same things before – it's because you probably have, and that's more than okay. Many of the books that I've mentioned in this one had similar messages. But it could have been in the wording, timing, context, or combination of thoughts that might have made a concept "click" for me and that's why I want to keep reading more – it's why we all should. Of course, you could have started reading this book and already knew everything I discussed in the first chapter's basic information, but I know you haven't read anything about angel employment™ and you were smart to keep reading. As you noticed, I love quotes because we get to pass on that information as perfectly as the original person expressed it.

Pray

I may not be, or at least have not been, as avid a reader as others, but I have read before about the power of prayer and have most certainly experienced it. I recommend the books by Stormie Omartian, including *The Power of a Praying Wife* and *The Power of a Praying Parent,* which I have. The series also includes *The Power of a Praying Husband,* and *The Power of a Praying Nation.* At the end of each chapter, Stormie provides "Power Tools" so, in the same spirit, here are a collection of Bible verses that I love, which have often appeared when I needed them and, hopefully, they can help you, too:

1. I can do all things through Christ who strengthens me. **Philippians 4:13**

2. There is no fear in love, because God's perfect love casts out fear. **1 John 4:18**

3. Fear not, for I am with you; be not dismayed, for I am your God; I will strengthen you, I will help you, I will uphold you with my righteous right hand. **Isaiah 41:10**

4. Do not be anxious about anything, but in every situation, by prayer and petition, with thanksgiving, present your requests to God. And the peace of God, which transcends all understanding, will guard your hearts and your minds in Christ Jesus. Finally, brothers and sisters, whatever is true, whatever is noble, whatever is right, whatever is pure, whatever is lovely, whatever is admirable—if anything is excellent or praiseworthy—think about such things. **Philippians 4:6-8**

5. Therefore, my beloved brothers, be steadfast, immovable, always abounding in the work of the Lord, knowing that in the Lord your labor is not in vain. **1 Corinthians 15:58**

6. Peace I leave with you; my peace I give you. I do not give to you as the world gives. Do not let your hearts be troubled and do not be afraid. **John 14:27**

7. When you pass through the waters, I will be with you; and when you pass through the rivers, they will not sweep over you. When you walk through the fire, you will not be burned; the flames will not set you ablaze. **Isaiah 43:2**

8. Be still, and know that I am God. **Psalm 46:10**

9. Be watchful, stand firm in the faith, act like men, be strong. Let all that you do be done in love. **1 Corinthians 16:13-14**

10. I sought the LORD, and he answered me; he delivered me from all my fears. Those who look to him are radiant; their faces are never covered with shame. This poor man called, and the LORD heard him; he saved him out of all his troubles. The angel of the LORD encamps around those who fear him, and he delivers them. Taste and see that the LORD is good; blessed is the one who takes refuge in him. **Psalms 34:4-8**

11. Our faith can move mountains. **Matthew 17:20**

12. And we know that in all things God works for the good of those who love him, who have been called according to his purpose. **Romans 8:28**

13. Trust in the Lord with all your heart, and do not lean on your own understanding. In all your ways acknowledge him, and he will make straight your paths. **Proverbs 3:5–6**

14. Do nothing from selfish ambition or conceit, but in humility count others more significant than yourselves. Let each of you look not only to his own interests, but also to the interests of others. **Philippians 2:3–4**

15. Give thanks to the Lord, for He is good; his love endures forever. **Psalm 107:1**

16. The steadfast love of the Lord never ceases; his mercies never come to an end; they are new every morning; great is your faithfulness. **Lamentations 3:22-23**

17. Now to him who is able to do immeasurably more than all we ask or imagine, according to his power that is at work within us. **Ephesians 3:20**

18. Jesus looked at them and said, 'With man it is impossible, but not with God. For all things are possible with God.' **Mark 10:27**

19. Go, eat rich foods and drink sweet drinks, and allot portions to those who had nothing prepared; for today is holy to our Lord. Do not be saddened this day, for rejoicing in the Lord is your strength! **Nehemiah 8:10**

20. For I know the plans I have for you," declares the LORD, "plans to prosper you and not to harm you, plans to give you hope and a future. **Jeremiah 29:11**

Listen

You may believe in a higher power, say God or the Universe. I, too, believe. No matter where I've been on my journey, there have been countless times when I've come across "signs" or messages that spoke right to my soul. Sometimes, they were whispers that took me a while to acknowledge. Other times, they came in loud and clear. It's always helpful to have reminders that keep us moving forward and, more importantly, to be actively listening to them. I found many of the quotes and messages I use to overcome fear in books and in social media.

Following the right people on social platforms is the same concept as surrounding yourself with positive influences, and they are great resources to help you overcome fear. You need to listen.

Conclusion

What comes after the motivational books, the books that help you build good habits, and the books that help you develop your technical skills? This book! As I mentioned, I wish I could teach someone how to overcome fear, but allow this book to help you put what you're afraid of aside. And, above anything else, know that someone is praying for your happiness and sending you positive energy. Much love to you today, and every day, from my family and me. May God **continue** to bless you.

ANGEL EMPLOYMENT™ EXPLAINED

"Be the change that you wish to see in the world." Mahatma Ghandi

One of my favorite quotes has been, *"When you're sleeping, I'm working and, when you're working, I'm working harder."* I don't know who said it, but I love this quote. It personifies the energy of the "hustle." What I didn't know back when I first heard it, though, whether it was because I was young or naïve, is that it is not possible, ideal, smart, nor necessary to work that much and that hard.

If I want to be financially free, then I need to be a business owner and/or investor. I need to have my money working for me while *I'm* sleeping or on vacation instead of continuing to slave away day in and day out on a job that pays me last, limits the amount of money I can make, requires my physical presence to generate income, and demands that I work longer and harder to make more. I still love this quote because I love the hustle but, instead, I see it from the perspective of my money now. As a business owner and investor, my money is working for me when I'm sleeping and, when I'm working, my money is working even harder.

Problem-Solving

Various books and people taught Farhad and me invaluable lessons, but it was up to us to apply what we learned. They told us to find a problem and solve it. Hopefully, you've gotten a better and more practical understanding of what people like me would have to go through to cross the bridge from employee to full-time entrepreneur. As Rory Vaden says, *"You are always most powerfully positioned to serve the person you once were."* Day Hustle™ provides employees the opportunity to break free from their golden handcuffs and to get on the fast track to financial freedom. Let's break down the case study:

- ◆ Gianna learned that working as an employee will not help her reach her goals, and that working for herself is the fastest way to being financially independent.

- ◆ Gianna loves writing, but only did it on the side when she had time (and energy). If she had the time to focus on writing and selling books, Gianna was confident that she could turn it into a business and make lots of money doing what she loves.

- ◆ Despite knowing these, Gianna was afraid of losing the benefits of her day job.

- Farhad was planning his next investments and considered investing in a few businesses. He decided to invest some of his money in funding a company called Day Hustle™.

- Day Hustle™ offered to provide Gianna all of the benefits she was used to from her day job for the purpose of Gianna growing a writing business full-time.

- Gianna quit her day job, formed a company, and called it Honeymoon Media.

- With Day Hustle™ supporting her, Gianna focused on growing Honeymoon Media.

- Gianna didn't have to worry about her household expenses and worked on her business at least eight hours a day. Within four months, she completed writing a book, marketed the book and launched it, and laid the groundwork for other income streams for Honeymoon Media, including a YouTube channel.

Day Hustle™ is the key to an employee's golden handcuffs. But angel employment™, as a new form of private equity/business investing, is also the solution to various problems that both business owners and investors are facing as well. Firstly, it is tough to be a business owner these days. The labor market is quite competitive as we go through the "Great Resignation." And people are not only leaving to go to what they may think is a better company. They are leaving for better opportunities. It is likely that your most successful employees are entrepreneurs with an idea and an itch to pursue that idea just waiting for the right opportunity. No one dreams of working for someone else forever. It could be their current plan, but only while they're "asleep." When they wake up and truly start dreaming, that dream will be about freedom, and true freedom means they have no boss but themselves. This said, imagine the number of employees you'll have knocking on your door if you gave them the greatest benefit of all – the time to do whatever *they* wanted.

And, if you are having any kind of problems with market competition, production, customer service, or business development, imagine if you didn't have anything to sell, no products to create, no services to perform, nor customers to attract. I, for one, love working with people, but not necessarily when they're customers. I love being in the service of others and helping them, but, again, not as customers. And we're all customers; *I'm* a customer. But we've been put on a pedestal with the "customer is always right" mentality and this has resulted in people with unreasonably high expectations and people thinking they are always right. A world without customers, but with partners and networks, is more ideal for me. This is what it's like for Day Hustle™.

Investing

According to *Investopedia*, an angel investor is someone who provides financial backing for small startups or entrepreneurs. The term "angel investor" was first used by William Wetzel, the founder of the Center for Venture Research, as part of his study on raising capital – it was used to describe wealthy individuals investing in Broadway theater to propel theatrical productions. I find it both fun and coincidental that the original angel employer™'s first day hustler™ chose a media company to propel (Honeymoon Media), and I hope that the term "angel employer™" will one day be added to *Investopedia's* dictionary, right before the term "angel investor."

Angel employment™ doesn't replace the need for angel investors (or any other type of seed funding). While angel investors finance the business expenses, angel employers™ take care of the day hustler™'s personal expenses so they can focus on growing their businesses and not worry about paying their mortgage or health insurance bill.

There is no better time than now to be investing in businesses and the growing number of entrepreneurs, but investing in businesses is risky, and angel investors stand to lose *all* their money if a business goes down. Various reports indicate 75% to 90% of startups fail; however, angel employment™ provides at least 33% more time in a day for founders to focus on their businesses, inherently increasing the startup's chance for success. *All* the other benefits that the day hustlers™ receive, as described in Chapter Six, improves the odds. We certainly can't guarantee the amount and speed of growth, but it stands to reason that an angel investor will be better off investing in a day hustler™'s business, as opposed to a business whose founder only does it on the side or with the distraction of covering their household expenses and the anxiety of uncertainty.

As a private equity/business investor, you can be an angel investor, or you can also consider being an angel employer™. Angel investing often requires a long waiting period before you start seeing any return of investment, let alone a return *on* your investment. As discussed in Chapter Six, the day hustler™ starts to pay Day Hustle™ back from the first month and Day Hustle™ will have recouped its total investment by the time the day hustler™ retires, whether after 18, 12, or only four months in. The Angel Capital Association performed a study and reported an average 27% Internal Rate of Return. Day Hustle™ plans result in a 35-45% yield! The cashflow can then be reinvested into other assets.

Angel employment™ is a way to diversify your investments without taking part in crowdfunding or putting all your eggs in one basket – it's a way to extend the reach of the money you have available to invest. Your investment in a particular business is not made in large lump sums, but rather in small injections via monthly or semi-monthly paychecks. I recommend twice-a-month paychecks on the first and fifteenth, simply because they are what I was used to as an employee, but also because they keep the payments for the angel employer™ smaller and make for easier accounting as it doesn't matter how many weeks there are in a particular month.

Personally, Farhad and I are self-diagnosed with ADHD. We enjoy working with startups because we can help get them going then turn them into passive income streams. While investing in businesses is high-risk, there is a great potential for high reward. There is no limit to the amount a business can make and, as an angel employer™, you have stakes in multiple companies long before their Initial Public Offering (IPO). Securing the controlling interest in the business until the day hustler™'s retirement also gives an angel employer™ collateral during the early stages.

Moreover, having an angel employment™ business is scalable. There are countless opportunities to generate more income streams. For example, you can further propel your day hustler™'s businesses by selling them books from which they can learn, by building an app that can make them more efficient, and by holding conferences and expos to build their network.

There are several advantages to being an angel employer™. As we evaluate Day Hustle™ candidates, we expect to get countless opportunities to read financial statements and analyze businesses, skills we want to continue developing. Moreover, we will be surrounding ourselves with like-minded people and experts in their respective fields, and we'll be sure to continue finding mentors along the way.

Take particular note of the network a day hustler™ will be part of as well. Knowing the right people, having connections, and supporting each other's businesses help everyone. Every business Day Hustle™ helps grow can service the other businesses, so money would be circling back to us. If a day hustler™ buys the products or uses the services of another day hustler™, then they both help each other, and the angel employer™ benefits from the increase in sales. It's not just about receiving help, but rather about helping each other – mutual benefits.

Day Hustle™ also helps us on a philosophical level. It takes leadership to be a successful business owner. But how can we lead employees if we believe that being one is not the way to go? We believe that being an employee is not a good option for anyone unless they're looking to learn. So if we want to continue being business owners or investing in businesses, how would we be good leaders for our employees? Day Hustle™ solves this quandary for us and allows us to encourage and/or lead people to building their own businesses.

Working Together

If this makes sense to you, and if you are interested in learning more about angel employment™ or day hustler™ candidates, then we've done all the legwork to get Day Hustle™ started and would be happy to share our resources as they become available for distribution, such as:

- ♦ Salary and profit tables
- ♦ Operating procedures
- ♦ Sample employment and securities agreements

- Payroll and benefits administration information
- Referrals

Please note that investments are currently limited to "accredited investors," defined by the Securities and Exchange Commission (SEC) as having a minimum $1M in net worth or earning at least $200k in the previous 2 years. The timing and structure of investment opportunities will vary. As our platforms are developed, you can request to be updated regarding investment opportunities, requirements, and available resources by going to angelemployers.com. As I mentioned in the Introduction, we have an opportunity to help millions of people grow successful businesses and live fulfilling lives, and we can do it together!

Acknowledgements

I want to give all the glory to God for blessing me with people that love, support, encourage, inspire, motivate, teach, and challenge me. Thank you to my family and chosen family near and far, friends and colleagues, mentors and role models, followers, and supporters. I am where I am today because of you, your influence, and your impact.

AUTHOR BIO

———⬦———

Gianna Marie Rahmani, often referred to as "G," is known first and foremost for her passionate love for, and devotion to, her husband, Farhad, and two boys, Nikolas and Dominik. G is the type of person you want in your corner, as she would do anything in her power to help those in need.

A Filipino-American, G immigrated to the US in 1990, when she was seven years old. She grew up in Secaucus, NJ and Ellicott City, MD, eventually moving to El Sobrante, CA where she met Farhad. There, G also started her career in property management, throughout which she would often write industry-related articles for blogs and magazines.

In school and in business, G has earned the respect of her peers for her amiability, positivity, maturity, versatility, creativity, and ingenuity, resulting in accolades such as Unsung

Hero, Scholar Athlete, Homecoming Queen, Rising Star, and Manager of the Year. She helped lead teams in winning seasons, smashing goals, earning awards, and reaching #1 rankings.

Regardless of the endeavor, G is always on the fast track to the top as team captain, director, committee chair, or board president. As a mentor or keynote speaker, G is always looking for ways to inspire and motivate through her words and by example.

Given her proven track record, it's no surprise that G retired at 39 from a highly successful 20-year career, now focusing on her and her husband's businesses and investments from warm and sunny Florida. It's no further surprise that G is pursuing her passion for writing to help others have happy and fulfilling lives and relationships. As an author, G is carrying out her personal mission to deliver a message of love through every word she speaks (or writes) and action she takes, reflective of her favorite F words – Family, Fun, Faith, Fitness, Food, Finances, Freedom, and Fulfillment. She is the other half of F&G – Farhad and Gianna.

It's rare to see a couple that is as close to each other as they are. F&G do everything together and are partners in every sense of the word, from being best friends and gym buddies, to being parents of two amazing boys and co-founders of several businesses. Together, F&G hustle to *The Honeymoon Life* – what they've characterized as a life focused on love and adventure, and one that you don't need a vacation from. They don't shy away from taking risks and making bold moves, as long as they have a plan, have faith, and do it together.

And they want to inspire others to do the same. As entrepreneurs and investors, they are the founders of Day Hustle™ and are recognized as the original angel employers™, helping employees to unlock their golden handcuffs of so-called job "security" and to get on the fast track to financial freedom.

www.ingramcontent.com/pod-product-compliance
Lightning Source LLC
Chambersburg PA
CBHW070355200326
41518CB00012B/2242